Navigating With Nerve

Assertive Strategies for Life

Linton J. Khor

Library of Congress Control Number: 2024922396

Table of Contents

*To all who saw the words within me before I did
– this is for you*

Introduction

In a world that often demands us to either roar or retreat, assertive communication is a powerful and transformative tool. Assertive communication is the art of expressing oneself honestly and respectfully while concurrently considering the rights and feelings of others. Not to be confused with the more commonly known passive and aggressive communication styles, assertive communication offers a pathway to more effective and harmonious interactions. This book is designed to help you develop this essential communication skill.

Imagine a conversation where your voice is heard and valued without overshadowing others. For many in today's world, this balance between hearing and being heard can seem nearly impossible to achieve. This was the case for Eleanor, a senior account manager at a prestigious advertising agency. As a client of mine several years ago, Eleanor was in dire need of effective communication methods at her job, especially when it came to balancing the weight of compassion and firmness. As we worked together to achieve her goals, Eleanor was able to grow her assertiveness into a functional, practical, and essential life skill.

The turning point for Eleanor was during a meeting at her agency. Facing a tight deadline from a high-profile client, Eleanor and her team were struggling to see eye-to-eye. The creative director wanted to push the boundaries with an edgy, unconventional campaign, while the marketing strategist pushed for a more traditional approach.

As frustrations rose and communication broke down, Eleanor saw an opportunity to showcase the techniques she had been working on. Cutting through the noise, she paused the meeting and regrouped everyone. Making eye contact with each member of her team, she instructed each person to state their desired approach, asking questions and validating each person's ideas. Ensuring that everyone in the meeting was heard, Eleanor was able to effectively facilitate a discussion without tensions boiling over.

When her team presented the new concept to the client, it was met with enthusiastic approval. The client appreciated the fresh approach that still honored their brand's core values. Eleanor's ability to navigate the discussion with nerve—balancing firmness with respect—had not only saved the project but also strengthened their team. As she walked into my office after the experience, she thanked me for all of the progress she had made. "I feel like I finally found my voice," she said.

A story like Eleanor's might seem miles out of reach; an ideal that most can only dream about. However, assertiveness is more achievable than you might think.

Picture a scenario where you can confidently set boundaries, express your needs, and handle conflicts with grace and dignity. These aren't just fantasies, they're achievable outcomes—provided you have the right tools and mindset.

Whether you're navigating personal relationships, workplace dynamics, or social settings, assertive communication empowers you to advocate for yourself while fostering mutual respect. It involves not just what you say, but how you say it, using body language, tone, and active listening to reinforce your words.

Throughout this book, you'll find practical strategies, real-world examples, and interactive exercises to help you develop and refine your assertive communication skills. You'll learn how to overcome common obstacles, such as a fear of confrontation, a lack of confidence, and ingrained habits of passive or aggressive behavior.

By embracing assertive communication, you open the door to improved relationships, enhanced self-esteem, and a more fulfilling life. Let this book be your companion as you discover the strength in your voice and the power of your words.

Welcome to the transformative journey of learning assertive communication: *Navigating With Nerve*. Your path to being heard, understood, and respected starts here.

Chapter 1:

Understanding Assertiveness

Assertiveness is often spoken about in the context of wider personality traits and pop psychology. To be clear, there's nothing inherently wrong with this. For decades, scientists, medical experts, and professionals from many schools of thought have sought to understand more about the way the mind works.

You might be familiar with popularized tests and assessments like the Myers-Briggs test, which assigns individuals a series of letters based on a spectrum of traits. If you're active on social media platforms like Instagram or TikTok, you may have also seen a rise in the use (and misuse) of therapy terms such as attention-deficit/hyperactivity disorder (ADHD), obsessive-compulsive disorder (OCD), borderline personality disorder

(BPD), and a range of other diagnoses that are commonly used to describe personality traits. While these are indeed official diagnoses defined in the DSM-5, many professionals, social media users, and creators also use them in an informal (and often medically incorrect) manner. Meanwhile, some people also express their personality traits through astrological signs, Hogwarts houses, or other supposedly telling personal preferences.

For anyone navigating the sea of self-improvement content out there, the possibilities for self-diagnoses can seem never-ending. A lot of the time, this array of definitions and diagnoses is rooted in either misinterpreted (or sometimes entirely fraudulent) science and typically lacks evidence to back it up.

According to University of Nevada Las Vegas professor Stephen Benning, a lot of these personality tests and labels encourage individuals to "take this very generic statement about universal human tendencies and somehow think it's uniquely applicable to them" (Haupt, 2024, p. 10). While some elements of pop psychology can help people begin to seek professional psychological help and destigmatize mental health problems, other parts can do more harm than good—especially if a particular label creates an archetype for behavior that aligns with the label.

The wariness around pop psychology and personality assessments has even spread to areas outside of pop culture. For some mental health and medical professionals, labels like introversion and extroversion are becoming less favorable (Kozak, 2014). As social media influences more and more of our daily lives, professionals are often worried about the effects that oversimplification and misinformation can have on our ideas of ourselves.

In this context, assertiveness can seem like just another trendy term. However, when we talk about assertiveness, we are *not* talking about social media fads or buzzwords. Instead, it's far more useful to think of assertiveness as a tool in your lifestyle toolkit—something you can pull out to neutralize stressful situations, heighten communication skills, and improve the quality of your relationships.

This tool is separate from you, a complex individual with depth and a wide array of life experiences. This is the approach that Dr. Arnie Kozak, clinical assistant professor of psychiatry at the University of Vermont College of Medicine, prefers when it comes to picking labels. Even for widespread concepts like introversion and extroversion, Kozak says, "There is still no such *thing* as an introvert. Thing implies a noun. Introverts and extroverts are not nouns, but verbs. Humans are always in the process of becoming; our thingness is an illusion" (Kozak, 2014, p. 2). This is often where social media and pop psychology fail the average person; labels are meant to fit you, not the other way around.

In keeping this separation between your psychological toolkit and yourself in mind, assertiveness becomes less of a hurdle and more of a unique opportunity for personal growth. No matter what labels you give yourself—introverted or extroverted, obsessive-compulsive or carefree, Gemini or Leo—assertiveness is a life skill that everyone can benefit from. There are no prerequisites for learning about assertive communication. As long as you are open to listening and willing to put yourself out there, assertiveness is well within your grasp.

What Is Assertiveness?

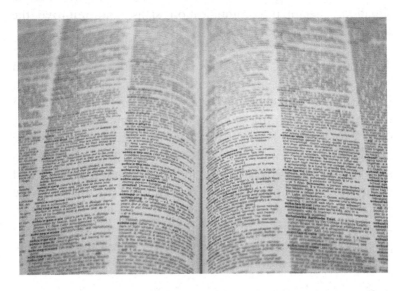

To kickstart your exploration into this new lifestyle tool, let's look at the word "assertiveness." On the surface, the definition of assertiveness seems simple enough. According to the Merriam-Webster dictionary being assertive is defined as being "disposed to or characterized by bold or confident statements and behavior" (Merriam-Webster, n.d.-a).

It seems simple, right? However, this definition, while helpful for beginners, doesn't dig deep enough into what assertiveness truly is in the modern-day context of personal psychology. While both characteristics play an important role, assertiveness is much more than just a combination of boldness and confidence. If increasing your self-confidence or your boldness was all there was to it, then we'd have no need for a term like "assertiveness."

History and context can help us fill in the gap between simple confidence and assertiveness. Using the dictionary definition as a diving board, let's explore further by briefly studying the etymology of the word. According to Merriam-Webster, the first known use of the word "assert" was recorded around the year 1604, taken from the Latin root *asserere*, or "to join."

This root, asserere, is also the source of many other English words, most notably the word "series." As you might have already been able to tell, the Latin root was originally used in the context of linking ideas, arguments, and opinions together into one coherent stream of thought. In the same way that you might present a story or a line of reasoning—in a logical series of events—one might also present information about themselves and their place in the world.

When *asserere* was taken into English as "assert," the original Latin definition was changed somewhat. This happened in two ways; "assert" began to gain some of the attributes of other English words like "forceful," especially in places like English courts of law where parties often made passionate assertions. For the same reason, the term was also influenced by other legal ideas such as the demonstration of evidence. As time went on, "assert" was adapted into different parts of speech, and according to research conducted by the Oxford English Dictionary, the noun "assertiveness" was first recorded in 1881 (Oxford English Dictionary, 2023).

Nowadays, if you look up the word "assertiveness" online, you'll find several definitions that closely mirror the Merriam-Webster definition. You'll also find dozens of synonyms, including words like "aggressive," "ambitious," and "fierce." When we talk about assertiveness as a life skill, this is *not* what we mean.

Rather than looking at simple dictionary definitions, we must reach through all of the layers of etymological history to discover the true meaning. The assertiveness that we're referring to does not imply aggression or pushiness. Instead, we can think of assertiveness as an act of self-demonstration; a logical series of details and facts that describe who you are to others, and a way of effectively connecting yourself with the world around you.

Conceptualizing the abstract idea of assertiveness is an important step in mastering it as a life skill, but it's also crucial to recognize what this means on a concrete level. Resolving to connect yourself with the world around you is a great starting point, but what does that actually look like on a day-to-day basis? The key to this lies in your relationships with the people around you.

The point of being assertive is to better express yourself, your needs, and your desires to others. With this in mind, the times when you interact with people should be the focal point of your efforts to be more assertive. Assertiveness doesn't happen in a bubble. You probably already have a good idea of who you are and what you want. The truly transformational element of assertiveness happens when you begin to externalize your thoughts, feelings, and needs in a genuine way. In essence, the most crucial aspects of assertiveness have to do with communicating effectively and honestly, standing your ground, and respecting (and sometimes respectfully disagreeing with) what other people say.

Assertiveness as a Tool for Communication

In today's world, miscommunications arise all the time. We're constantly surrounded by misunderstandings and communicative mishaps, many of which result in unexpected—and sometimes undesirable—outcomes.

To illustrate this, let's take a look at a couple of real-life examples. On the popular social media platform X, users often describe their most amusing debacles, many of which revolve around crucial yet subtle miscommunications. In a 2020 post, one user wrote: "Husband and I reminiscing about the time I texted him on my way home: 'Can you start cooking those sausages?' Then added <3 as a cute little heart. He cooked two sausages." (Keturka & Laurinavicius, 2020, p. 2). Another user detailed a similar food-related incident, writing, "on a shopping list - next to fruit and veg, I write 'check dates'. My husband comes home with a beautiful box of Moroccan dates" (Keturka & Laurinavicius, 2020, p. 15). One user recalled a story that many parents will likely relate to; "This reminds me of the mother who while reversing out of a car space asked her son, 'are there any cars coming?' to which he replied, 'no'. Then after a slight pause, 'but there is a truck'" (Keturka & Laurinavicius, 2020, p. 13).

Hilarious stories like these are practically never-ending on social media platforms, perhaps because misunderstandings in real life are similarly never-ending. As you might've noticed, none of these tales imply a right or wrong party, per se. Rather, the characters in these stories are simply operating on different levels. These gaps can come from a variety of places, though miscommunications usually stem from differences in understandings, approaches, or intentions when it comes to dealing with an ambiguous situation. Depending on your personality, background, skills, and a plethora of other factors, you won't always see eye-to-eye with other people, inevitably yielding a miscommunication of some kind.

Given that we are all unique and individual thinkers, miscommunications between people will never cease to exist. This ultimately comes down to a struggle between two worlds: your internal world, full of worries, emotions, and thoughts, and the external world.

Unfortunately for many of us, this relationship is a one-way street, so to speak. That is, you can observe your surroundings, but the people you interact with can't read your mind. When other people don't have enough information, they will typically rely on what information they *do* know, which may be very different from your intended message.

We can briefly summarize this struggle as intent versus perception, or your intended message versus how others receive what you're saying. According to Heidi Grant Halvorson, a psychologist at Columbia Business School, solving the issue of intent versus perception means that "it's much more practical for you to decide to be a good sender of signals," rather than counting on others to infer your intent. "Can you imagine how exhausting it would be to weigh every possible motivation of another person?" (Smith, 2015, p. 25).

With this in mind, we can better understand the inverse scenario. In other words, we can't assume that everyone communicates effectively all the time. This is why true assertiveness also requires you to drop any snap judgments you might have about others, instead of relying on observable behavior.

It's this exact dilemma—the eternal struggle between what goes on in our heads and what goes on in the world around us—that assertive communication attempts to resolve. By clearly stating what you want, sticking to your word, and communicating honestly, openly, and empathetically, you can help eliminate many of the miscommunications that hold you back from truly interacting with the world. On the flip side, remaining nonjudgmental, impartial, and honest about what others communicate to you can help minimize miscommunication even more.

The Benefits of Being Assertive

Mastering the skill of assertiveness can improve your life in a variety of ways. In one comprehensive study published in the *Journal of Health, Medicine and Nursing*, researchers found that, among those who occupied high-stress and highly communicative jobs like nursing, participants with assertive communication styles reported far higher rates of satisfaction after interpersonal communication Additionally, nurses who interacted with those who possessed assertive communication styles were also more likely to come away feeling satisfied with the interaction. Those who didn't possess assertive styles, however, reported far higher rates of dissatisfaction after talking with others (Kaur & S.K, 2015).

According to the authors of the study, this correlation between assertiveness and interpersonal satisfaction can happen for a variety of reasons (Kaur & S.K, 2015):

- More stable emotional states over time due to assertiveness.

- The ability to say "no" without feelings of shame or guilt.

- The ability to recognize one's own positive and negative qualities in a healthy way.

- A stronger sense of self-worth, self-esteem, and confidence.

The last point is an important, yet paradoxical one. Assertiveness supports and is supported by your self-image. The two concepts reinforce each other, with self-esteem shoring up assertiveness and vice versa.

Adopting an assertive communication style allows you to express your thoughts, feelings, and needs clearly and confidently, which significantly boosts your self-esteem. When you stand up for yourself and set boundaries, you cultivate a sense of self-respect and personal integrity. This newfound confidence positively impacts all areas of your life, enabling you to interact with others from a place of strength and assurance. By consistently practicing assertive communication, you become more comfortable with expressing your true self, which reinforces your confidence and helps you to face challenging situations with greater ease.

That's all well and good, but are there any immediate material benefits to adopting assertiveness? As it turns out, yes! A consistently assertive communication style also lends itself to a variety of other benefits:

- Improving your interpersonal relationships. Assertiveness fosters mutual respect in relationships, as both parties feel heard and valued. Clear and honest communication helps prevent misunderstandings and reduces the likelihood of conflicts escalating. This creates a more harmonious and supportive environment where relationships can thrive, whether with friends, family, or colleagues. By communicating assertively, you can address issues directly and constructively, leading to stronger, more resilient relationships. This approach also encourages others to be open and honest with you, further enhancing mutual trust and understanding.

- Boosting your decision-making skills. When you communicate assertively, you articulate your thoughts and opinions with clarity, aiding in more effective decision-making processes. Assertiveness enhances your negotiation skills by allowing you to clearly state your needs while considering the needs of others. This balanced approach leads to better, more inclusive decisions. By confidently expressing your viewpoints and listening to others, you can gather more information and perspectives, which helps in making well-informed decisions. Additionally, assertiveness helps you to advocate for the best solutions and gain support from others, leading to more successful outcomes.

- Helping you find greater professional success. Assertive individuals are often seen as leaders who can communicate effectively and manage teams with confidence. Being able to advocate for yourself and your ideas can lead to greater recognition and opportunities for career growth. This professional success is driven by the ability to interact with colleagues and superiors in a clear, respectful, and confident manner. Assertiveness enables you to navigate workplace dynamics more effectively, handle feedback constructively, and address challenges proactively. As a result, you are more likely to achieve your professional goals and build a positive reputation in your field.

- Strengthening your emotional and mental well-being. Expressing yourself openly and honestly through assertive communication reduces the internal stress and frustration that often accompany passive or aggressive communication styles. This approach is a key component of emotional intelligence, helping you manage your emotions and respond to others' emotions more effectively, contributing to overall emotional well-being. By addressing issues as they arise and maintaining open lines of communication, you can prevent emotional build-up and reduce anxiety. This leads to a healthier emotional state, where you feel more in control of your feelings and interactions.

- Boosting your sense of autonomy. Assertive communication empowers you to take control of your life and make decisions that align with your values and needs. By encouraging personal responsibility for your actions and choices, assertiveness leads to a greater sense of autonomy. This empowerment allows you to navigate life with confidence and purpose. By clearly expressing your desires and setting boundaries, you create a life that reflects your true self and priorities. This sense of control over your life decisions fosters a deeper sense of satisfaction and fulfillment, as you are actively shaping your own destiny.

- Setting healthy boundaries in all areas of your life. Setting and maintaining healthy boundaries is a crucial benefit of assertive communication. By learning to say "no" and prioritize your needs, you can protect your time, energy, and emotional well-being. This proactive boundary setting helps you avoid overcommitting and experiencing burnout, leading to a more balanced and fulfilling life. By clearly defining what you are willing to accept and what you are not, you can prevent others from taking advantage of you. This respect for your own limits not only enhances your well-being but also encourages others to respect your boundaries.

- Providing you with an effective method of conflict resolution. Assertive communication promotes constructive dialogue and problem-solving, leading to more effective conflict resolution. By encouraging open and honest discussions, it helps in finding solutions that are beneficial for all parties involved, rather than one-sided outcomes. This approach ensures conflicts are resolved in a healthy and productive manner. Assertiveness allows you to address issues directly, express your needs and concerns, and listen to others' perspectives. This collaborative problem-solving process leads to more sustainable and agreeable resolutions, fostering a more positive environment.

- Allowing your true authenticity and integrity to shine. Engaging in assertive communication allows for more genuine and authentic interactions, fostering trust and transparency. It helps you align your actions and communication with your core values, leading to a more fulfilling and authentic life. This authenticity strengthens your relationships and ensures that your interactions are based on honesty and respect. By being true to yourself and expressing your thoughts and feelings openly, you build deeper connections with others. This integrity in communication helps you to create a life that is in harmony with your values and beliefs, leading to a greater sense of personal fulfillment and happiness.

These effects impact all areas of your life, from personal relationships to professional success. Even the smallest change in your mindset can send ripples out to every corner of your life, improving the quality of your communication and forever changing how you engage with the people around you. (And yourself!)

Unfortunately, we're not given a handbook detailing step-by-step instructions on how to interact with the world. In fact, many of us were never actually properly taught how to be assertive in a way that's actually effective. If you're like me, you probably used to think that assertiveness was the same as aggression and that communicating so directly was a surefire way to achieve confrontation.

Despite these misconceptions, assertiveness is actually a lifelong tool that can yield some remarkable results. In the next chapter, we'll take a closer look at assertiveness and some of the alternatives, as well as the psychology and science that back up their efficacy.

Chapter 2:

The Assertiveness Spectrum

In the last chapter, we touched a little bit on the power (and pitfalls) of labels. Used correctly, labels can help you find new solutions, mindsets, and frameworks for success that are catered to your lifestyle. Used incorrectly, labels can quickly become boxes that inhibit your personal growth and trap you in unhelpful cycles of thinking. Despite the potential to do more harm than good, we're still forced to put names to ideas and concepts. The transition from names to labels is a subtle one, and sometimes we don't even know that it's happening.

In the world of self-improvement, it's worth questioning the names and labels we assign to things. As new ideas and words enter our lexicons, they begin to change how we see the world as a whole, from events that happen in our lives all the way to our self-perception.

That may sound like a bit of an exaggeration, but there are actually entire scientific fields that examine this exact phenomenon. As we grapple with the complexities of the human brain, a large portion of the scientific community has strived to better define the link between us and our language. Research in this area can sometimes become challengingly abstract and cerebral, so I find it more useful to look at real-world instances of how our use of labels can impact our lives.

A perfect example of this is something that we mentioned in the last chapter: astrology. More specifically, Chinese astrology.

Just in case you're not familiar with Chinese astrology, let's break it down. Like Western astrology, the Chinese Zodiac has 12 signs represented by animals. The Chinese Zodiac differs from Western astrology, however, in that the seasons of the signs last for an entire year.

One's sign is based on the year they were born. This is supposed to signify several different personality traits. For instance, people born in the year of the Ox are thought to be especially honest, thoughtful, determined, and loyal, while those born in the year of the Monkey are thought to be especially charming, funny, and outgoing.

It's often believed that the best year for a child to be born is the year of the Dragon, which symbolizes courage, intelligence, passion, and wisdom. Chinese children usually know their signs from the time they're young. As a result, they typically grow up with these astrological archetypes in the background of their everyday lives.

The year 1988 was the year of the Dragon, which made many expectant Chinese families very happy. After this generation of Dragon children was born, a pair of researchers from Louisiana

State University (LSU) looked into the effects that some signs—and the archetypes and expectations the signs carry—had on children as they grew up. More specifically, they examined the 1988 Dragon children as they progressed through school.

The outcome was surprising. Despite record classroom numbers, fewer resources, and extreme levels of competition to get into top schools and universities, Dragon children performed better in school across the board. From middle school tests to university entrance exams, these Dragon children were noticeably more advanced in their studies than their peers who had been born in other years (Vedantam, 2017).

This wasn't because Dragon children were naturally smarter or more academically gifted than other children, researchers discovered. Dragon children outperformed their peers because they had been told—by teachers, parents, and society at large—that they must succeed (Vedantam, 2017). The label of "dragon" was so strong that an entire generation of kids managed to score extremely well in their academic studies!

This isn't an isolated instance, either. Time and time again, researchers continue to find that the power of labels, both self-imposed and otherwise, impacts our lives in very real and meaningful ways. In 1968, researchers Robert Rosenthal and Lenore Jacobson published a study titled "Pygmalion in the Classroom: Teacher Expectation and Pupils' Intellectual Development," examining this exact phenomenon. In the experiment, first-grade teachers were told that a handful of students in their classes were especially gifted, even though the students were actually of average intelligence. Rosenthal and Jacobson tracked these "gifted" children all the way through high school, monitoring their academic outcomes, social lives, and other benchmarks for success. Their findings were nearly identical to those of the LSU researchers 20 years after them.

Children who had been labeled "gifted" at a young age were far more likely to find success in their academic careers compared to their peers, despite the fact that they hadn't shown any special characteristics (Rosenthal & Jacobson, 1968). Both then and now, the Pygmalion effect is alive and thriving in our collective consciousness.

As we continue to use labels in today's world, it's crucial to keep the Pygmalion effect in mind. When we navigate the tricky world of psychology, we must continue to interrogate which labels we use, why, and the possible outcomes they might produce—especially when it comes to learning new labels.

Labels Across the Assertiveness Spectrum

With this in mind, let's explore a more comprehensive perspective of assertiveness. As we all know, communication never happens in a vacuum. Misunderstandings abound, and you're inevitably going to come across people who have different backgrounds, ideas, and perspectives than you.

Not all interactions happen in a naturally assertive way, and we don't always communicate the way that we want to. Sometimes we aren't as patient or empathetic as we want to be, or maybe we compromise on things that are very important to us. This is part of the reason why the dictionary definition of "assertive" doesn't always work in our favor; there is a range of behaviors and outcomes that assertiveness can cover, and a blanket definition can drastically oversimplify what it means to be assertive in real life.

The labels we are about to explore will help us better understand what to aim for and what to avoid, to get the most out of our daily interactions. To do this, we need to look at what makes for good and bad interactions. Consider the image below:

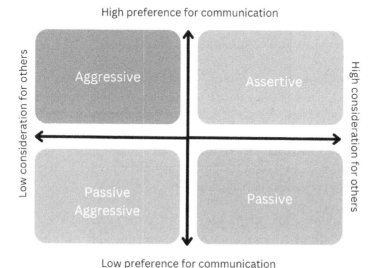

The two axes, consideration for others and openness to communication, are the two metrics that we're going to focus on for now.

As we learned in Chapter 1, assertiveness doesn't require you to have any skills or traits. This is something to keep in mind as you learn more about how to incorporate assertiveness into your personal style of communication.

Keeping in line with this sentiment, openness to communication doesn't mean that you have to be bubbly or extroverted all the time, and high consideration for others doesn't mean that you have to be friends with everyone. Rather, these metrics are designed to indicate two things: how willing you are to express yourself, and how much you care about the people you talk to. These two factors are crucial to assertiveness. Lacking in either of these areas can lead you further away from communicating assertively.

In an ideal world, we would always be able to communicate assertively by having both a high consideration for others as well as a high preference for communication. In the real world, this balancing act can be tough to master. Even people who are typically considered social butterflies can struggle to be both conscientious and communicative in their day-to-day lives.

If you look at the topics "assertive" or "assertiveness" on internet forums like Quora or Reddit, you'll find pages upon pages of advice, research, and personal experience detailing the trials and tribulations that arise as people try to become more assertive. In one such forum post, one user expressed something very common among people who want to increase their assertiveness (Chang, 2016, p. 2):

> For a lot of my life, I've been a very passive person, afraid to speak up when someone did me dirty. But over the past few years (when I've really started to

embrace speaking up), I've shifted to the other end of the spectrum where I sometimes wonder whether I'm too outspoken and confrontational.

There's no clear-cut way to be assertive, nor is the path to assertiveness easy. However, learning more about what to prioritize and what to steer clear of in your daily life is the first step in embracing your unique brand of assertiveness. To give you an idea of what the assertiveness spectrum looks like, let's explore some of the unfortunate alternatives that can arise when we aren't careful.

Passive Behavior

When you consider the word "passive," you might think of traits like shyness, introversion, or reservedness. As we discussed before, however, the synonyms that turn up in a quick Google search don't necessarily mean the same thing as the original word. For our purposes, passivity doesn't simply mean shyness or reservation. In this case, the Merriam-Webster definition of the word "passive" is actually pretty close to what we want; "acted upon by an external agency: receptive to outside impressions or influences: lacking in energy or will: receiving or enduring without resistance" (Merriam-Webster, n.d.-b).

The kind of passivity we're talking about indeed includes things like impressionability, external influence, and in some cases, a lack of agency. But, we can still get more specific than this using our two metrics, conscientiousness and communication.

Referring back to the chart above, passive behavior is characterized by a high consideration for others and a low inclination for communication. In and of themselves, these aren't necessarily bad traits to have. There are certainly times when you may not feel like talking, and ideally, we would all have a high consideration for others. However, the lack of communication in this case is where problems may start to arise. In the real world, passive behavior can be inconvenient at best, and potentially dangerous at worst.

Let's take a common example to illustrate how a low preference for communication can impact you in a minor way. Imagine the following scenario:

You're in a coffee shop. It's rush hour, and the shop is very loud and crowded. When you get to the counter, you relay your order to the barista, pay, and then wait for your coffee. When your order comes out, you notice that it's not what you asked for, even though your name is written on the side of the cup.

A person with a passive style of communication will probably hesitate to send back the coffee. After all, it's rush hour, and the baristas are likely overworked and stressed enough as it is. This is the conscientiousness metric in play, in which one might have a very high consideration for others.

In the same breath, a passive person will also compare their need for an exact coffee order against the needs of the workers and patrons of the coffee shop. In other words, a person with passive behaviors will rank their needs and desires lower than the needs and desires of everyone else. This effectively fulfills the low preference for communication. If you're okay with anything, then there's nothing to speak up about! In all likelihood, a person with a passive communication style will likely take the coffee, even though it wasn't what they wanted.

This scenario is a minor inconvenience in the grand scheme of things. As observers, we could write this kind of behavior off as that of a laid-back person, or maybe as that of a person who's just too busy to care much about something as menial as coffee. However, this passive communication style becomes more apparent when we look at different, more serious situations.

We may not always realize it, but we come across potentially dangerous situations all the time. In fact, those with more passive tendencies can even create these situations for themselves, sometimes unintentionally. To demonstrate this, imagine the following scenario from the perspective of a person with a passive communication style:

You're at a backyard party with a big group of friends and acquaintances. You're having a great time, and everyone is happily chatting over drinks and snacks. Everything seems perfectly fine until you start to feel a tightness across your chest. Even though this feels serious, you write it off as indigestion and you go back to talking. The tight feeling continues, growing worse as you try to keep chatting with your friends. No one has noticed how uncomfortable you are, and you think it would be a shame to break up the party because of something so minor. You don't want to bother anyone, so you decide that you'll just wait for the feeling to go away.

When we consider it from a bird's eye view, the potential danger to your health seems clear in this scenario. Sudden chest tightness can point to many different medical emergencies. Even if it's not a medical emergency, the principle remains— instead of speaking up when feeling uncomfortable, the person in this scenario would prefer to remain at the party despite their discomfort.

People with passive communication styles often struggle to recognize the importance of their own wants and needs. This passivity leads to prioritizing the needs of others, sometimes at their own expense. Ultimately, they may forfeit their own needs to accommodate others.

Most of the time, the consequences of this kind of communication are small. However, when we extrapolate passivity to problems outside of ourselves, it's clear that the toll of passive communication is far higher than a wrong coffee order. From dogs left in hot cars to speaking out against systemic oppression and societal wrongs, there are plenty of situations in which we—as bystanders—can't afford to be passive.

Aggressive Behavior

Circling back to our metrics of communication and conscientiousness, we can think of aggression as the complete opposite of passivity. In other words, aggressive communication styles have a very high preference for communication but a very low consideration for others.

Merriam-Webster defines the word "aggression" as "a forceful action or procedure (such as an unprovoked attack) especially when intended to dominate or master: the practice of making attacks or encroachments: hostile, injurious, or destructive behavior or outlook especially when caused by frustration" (Merriam-Webster, n.d.-c). This falls in line with what we know—that aggression stems from a lack of conscientiousness, or even sometimes from an outright disdain for other people.

Chances are that you've probably encountered this communication style at some point in your life. In an increasingly polarized and individualized world, we see aggressive communicators all the time, from national politics to road rage, aggressiveness toward others is everywhere.

On the flip side, aggressive communicators may often feel like aggression is the only way to express the strong emotions they feel toward a particular person, topic, or idea. Where passive communication places the wants and needs of others above one's own, aggressive communication prioritizes one's wants and needs above those of everyone else. This mindset may sometimes get you what you want, but it will also hurt those around you and burn all of your interpersonal bridges, so to speak. As you might imagine (and as we often see in the real world), aggressive behavior is not an effective way to communicate.

To see this in action, let's go back to the example of the coffee shop that we looked at earlier. Upon receiving a wrong coffee order, a person with a very aggressive communication style might yell to get a barista's attention, or they might try to dominate the physical space around them by cutting everyone else in line to demand a new coffee. Unlike someone with a passive communication style, an aggressive communicator couldn't care less about the other people in the coffee shop, instead prioritizing their own immediate needs.

This communication style is one of the oldest and most potent in the history of our species. Research has historically told us that aggressiveness comes from physical or emotional stimuli that trigger our fight-or-flight response. Like other animals, humans become aggressive when presented with threats, like predators, physical or psychological needs, and social conflict.

The physical circuitry in our brain that's responsible for this is called the hypothalamic attack area, more commonly known in pop psychology as the "lizard brain." Scientists discovered this back in the 1920s, when researcher Walter Hess began experimenting on different animal brains using electrodes (Fields, 2019).

Since then, we've uncovered a lot more about how the brain works. Researchers can now single out five brain regions that are responsible for aggressive responses in humans:

- The amygdala is an almond-shaped area responsible for fear-based emotions, anger, and detecting potential threats around us.

- The hypothalamus regulates hormones and controls many of our basic functions like body temperature, eating, and aggression.

- The limbic system connects all of our different brain regions.

- The pituitary gland releases stimuli-based hormones that control our fight-or-flight mode.

- The prefrontal cortex controls our ability to make complex decisions, focus on problems, and control our emotional impulses.

The neurological process of communicating aggressively also incorporates elements from other areas of the brain, like memory. Interestingly, according to research published in *Scientific American,* biological males tend to be far more prone to aggressive communication as a result of several biological factors (Fields, 2019). Some posit that this is why we tend to see more men in jail than women, though this claim hasn't been studied due to how complicated the criminal justice system can be. That being said, those of all genders can be prone to aggressive communication if they experience things that stimulate brain areas like the amygdala.

In relatively harmless—but nonetheless unpleasant—situations like the coffee debacle we looked at earlier, aggressive communication is perceived as rude but typical. However, overall aggressiveness can build up over time, leading to more dangerous situations if left unaddressed. In the worst cases, aggressive communication is a precursor to outright anger or even violence. This, of course, is not the ideal way to communicate.

Passive Aggressive Behavior

As discussed in the last chapter, pop psychology tends to misuse terms quite a bit. While social media platforms like TikTok and Instagram have sped up this process, the misuse of psychological terminology predates modern technology. Perhaps the best example of this is passive-aggressive behavior, formerly known as passive-aggressive personality disorder, or PAPD. The history of this categorization is a fascinating reflection of how the general public interacts with—and ultimately influences—the field of psychology, particularly when we misuse or change the meaning of certain labels.

The history of our understanding of passive-aggressive behavior started shortly after the end of the Second World War, during which time American scientists were looking for a new, comprehensive way to help returning soldiers with their mental health. More specifically, there wasn't a universal framework for diagnosing and treating mental illnesses or psychological conditions, which made it difficult for individual physicians to make diagnoses.

To help solve this problem, psychiatrists created the *Diagnostic and Statistical Manual of Mental Disorders* in 1952, colloquially known as the *DSM*. The original *DSM* included a general framework for identifying passive-aggressiveness, defined as aggression expressed "by passive measures, such as pouting, stubbornness, procrastination, inefficiency, and passive obstruction" (Lane, 2009. pg. 61).

As you might imagine, this first iteration of labeling passive aggression didn't actually help all that much. After all, if "stubbornness" was a symptom of a personality disorder, then mid-century hospitals would be filled with angsty teenagers! Later versions of the *DSM* tried to improve the definition, but ultimately failed to provide an adequate description of passive aggression as anything other than "stubbornness."

This is partially because of how quickly Americans adopted the term into everyday use. Passive-aggressive behavior was originally coined to describe the behavior of some young men in the military, particularly concerning their attitudes toward authority figures. As the term entered mainstream vernacular and was quickly applied to everyday people, however, passive aggression was considered less of a mental condition and more of a set of personality traits. When we hear the term "passive-aggressive" nowadays, most of us no longer think of military servicemen.

Using our metrics of communication and conscientiousness, passive-aggressive behavior scores pretty low on both axes. In other words, people who have a passive-aggressive communication style tend to have a low preference for communication and a low consideration for others. This is usually characterized by petty or catty behavior like:

- backhanded compliments

- the silent treatment

- sabotage disguised as an accident

- refusing or avoiding activities

To see this in action, let's go back to our coffee shop example. A person with a very passive-aggressive communication style would probably not ask for another coffee, nor would they tell the barista that their order was made incorrectly. Instead, they would likely do something simultaneously indirect and rude, like throwing away the wrong order and taking someone else's coffee instead. (And then leaving the shop a bad review from behind the comfort of their phone screen.)

Assertive Behavior

With the background of all the other labels on the assertiveness spectrum, we can better appreciate what good, effective communication looks like. Assertiveness, of course, is the best possible course of action in all forms of communication. With a high preference for communication and a high consideration for others, assertive behavior lets you externalize your true feelings while still keeping the needs and wants of others in mind. Assertive communication is honest but kind, empathetic but firm, and open but committed to your own needs.

Of course, this is often easier said than done. We all have natural preferences when it comes to communication. While you cognitively know that assertiveness is the best way to communicate, you may still struggle to comport your behavior accordingly.

There is some level of danger in forcing yourself into a box you don't fit into. As we discussed in the last chapter, this is a risk that all labels tend to carry. Luckily for us, this isn't what assertiveness aims to do.

As always, there are no prerequisites or particular traits that you need to become more assertive. As we'll soon discover in the following chapters, there isn't a cut-and-dry way to be assertive. Rather than contort yourself to fit an archetypal mold of assertiveness or confidence, you must find your own way forward as you progress on your journey to communicate effectively. This can be a challenging process, even for some of the most accomplished people out there. In the words of Lisa Earle McLeod, author of *The Triangle of Truth* (McLeod, 2012, p. 12):

> I spent much of my life with people telling me to chill out. It wasn't until someone said, 'Don't deny your energy, channel it,' that I finally realized: I'm never

going to be a low-key person. Nor do I even want to be. But I can be a focused person. You don't have to abandon the whole range of behaviors. When you have clarity on the nuance, you can step into the version that works for you.

In a world of oversimplified pop psychology terms, nuance is exactly what we want to shoot for. Assertiveness is not one-size-fits-all, but rather a lifestyle choice that we each must adapt for ourselves. In the next chapter, we'll study the foundations of assertiveness, as well as some of the inner work that can better support you on your assertive communication journey.

Chapter 3:

Building the Foundation for

Assertiveness

If you've ever played sports or participated in a physical activity class, you've probably experienced a strange phenomenon—you suddenly become aware of things that used to be automatic or natural. For instance, you might become aware of your posture, the way that you walk, or your breathing patterns. This sudden bodily awareness is sometimes called *sensorimotor obsession* by mental health professionals, and it can be a bit unnerving once you become aware of it. Sensorimotor awareness or obsession can trigger feelings of anxiousness for some, while others may focus more on correcting what they perceive to be wrong.

What does this have to do with growing your assertiveness, you might ask? Well, the first part of personal growth is gaining awareness of your current behaviors, tendencies, and traits. Now that you're investing time into improving your interpersonal skills, you may begin to see some behaviors that you've never noticed in yourself before. Just like with sensorimotor obsession, you might find yourself fixating on one or more aspects of your behavior, particularly when it comes to communication or mindset.

This is a natural—and necessary!—process, but it can definitely be uncomfortable at times. As you peel back the layers of your behavior, mindset, and personality, and as you become increasingly aware of yourself, you might find that the person you believe yourself to be isn't always the person you come across as.

As you might be able to tell, this kind of awareness is not innate for humans. We weren't born with the ability to read other people's minds or see ourselves from a distance. This makes the realization of awareness all the more jarring. In 2013, IDOLOGY founder and CEO Caroline McHugh spoke about the revelation of self-awareness through a true mirror. A true mirror, as she describes, is actually two mirrors that have been attached at right angles, which allows viewers to see themselves as others see them in their daily lives. In McHugh's words (McHugh, 2013, 2:37):

The difference is, when you look in a regular mirror, you look for reassurance. You look for reassurance that you're beautiful, or you're young, or you're tidy...But when you look in a true mirror, you don't look at yourself. You look for yourself. You look for revelation, not for reassurance.

In the process of gaining self-awareness, it's important to remember that growth isn't always comfortable. In all likelihood, you won't find much reassurance when you start to analyze your behavior. You will, however, uncover a new sense of zeal as you venture further down the path of self-discovery.

Self-Awareness and Self-Esteem

In the next part of your journey towards building assertiveness, self-awareness and self-esteem will be important tools in your mental toolbox. First, let's define what these terms mean:

- **Self-awareness** is the conscious knowledge of one's character, feelings, motives, and desires. It involves the ability to reflect on and understand one's thoughts, emotions, and behaviors, and how they align with one's values and goals. It enables individuals to recognize their strengths and weaknesses, understand how others perceive them, and make informed decisions based on this understanding.

- **Self-esteem** is the overall subjective evaluation of one's worth or value. It encompasses beliefs about oneself, such as "I am competent," or "I am worthy," as well as emotional states, such as triumph, despair, pride, and shame. High self-esteem involves having a positive view of oneself and feeling confident in one's abilities, whereas low self-esteem involves having a negative view of oneself and feeling inadequate or unworthy. Self-esteem is influenced by various factors, including personal experiences, relationships, and social interactions, and it plays a significant role in mental health and well-being.

It's important to note here that all of these factors that we've mentioned so far—assertiveness, self-esteem, and self-awareness—aren't necessarily isolated characteristics. In other words, all of these concepts interact with each other in a meaningful way. Self-awareness and self-esteem reinforce each other, which then in turn reinforces your sense of assertiveness.

As a result, we can view self-esteem and self-awareness as a kind of base of operations for your self-growth goals, or a diving board that can launch you more easily into healthy and assertive behaviors. Developing both self-awareness and self-esteem in a long-term, sustainable way will make assertive communication far less of a hurdle in your day-to-day interactions.

Self-Awareness in the Context of Assertiveness

In the discussion about self-awareness, you might find yourself wondering How can any of us aspire to see ourselves objectively? Aren't our perceptions of ourselves naturally biased?

The answer to both of these questions, of course, is yes. The question of objectivity is something that everyone will struggle with at one point or another. Whether it's a serious question about your behavior or something as simple as an outfit you're wearing, the question of self-perception versus other's perceptions will pervade your decision-making process. While we will always be naturally biased in our views of ourselves, there are several ways we can bring our biased perceptions closer to reality.

Researcher and New York Times bestselling author Tasha Eurich has studied self-awareness for years, especially as it pertains to our personal relationships and professional presence. According to her findings, developing self-awareness can empirically improve other aspects of your life such as (Eurich, 2018):

- confidence

- creativity

- good decision-making

- relationship strength

- professional outcomes

- leadership

Before we can see any of these benefits, however, we first have to grapple with the complexities of what it means to see yourself. According to Eurich (Eurich, 2018), there are two main areas of self-awareness that we can define clearly: internal self-awareness, or the clarity with which we know ourselves, and external self-awareness, or the extent to which we can see ourselves from the perspectives of others.

With these two axes in tow, Eurich developed a chart with four self-awareness archetypes: introspectors, seekers, pleasers, and fully aware individuals. This works similarly to the chart from the last chapter, with either high or low scores along the two axes (Eurich, 2018):

	Low external awareness	High external awareness
High internal awareness	**Introspectors**	**Full awareness**
Low internal awareness	**Seekers**	**Pleasers**

Introspectors know themselves very well but have trouble figuring out how they seem to others. Pleasers know how they seem to others, but sometimes have trouble with figuring out what they want. Seekers are those who don't have particularly high scores on either axis.

Ideally, we would have both high internal and external awareness, and these awarenesses would match each other. For most people, however, self-awareness is a difficult thing to accomplish and maintain. According to Eurich's research, which looked at sets of around 5,000 people across 10 different studies, only about 10%-15% of people exhibit self-awareness in their daily lives. This was the result even though most of the study participants believed themselves to be self-aware (Eurich, 2018).

When it comes to communicating assertively, both aspects of self-awareness are key. After all, how can you communicate your wants and needs to others if you don't fully understand them yourself?

Steps to Building Self-Awareness

Building self-awareness takes willpower, conscious effort, and most of all, it takes time. A simple journaling session won't do it! While there's nothing wrong with introspection, Eurich says, it's not as effective as we might think: "The problem with introspection isn't that it is categorically ineffective - it's that most people are doing it incorrectly" (Eurich, 2018, p. 21). When we engage in self-lead activities like journaling, there's nothing to stop introspection from turning into rumination, which can then lead us into a spiral of all of our perceived flaws.

Let's look at an example to illustrate how we might lead ourselves astray when we try to reflect in this way. Say that you messed up a presentation at work—you fumbled over your words, you didn't engage your audience like you wanted to, and nothing you tried seemed to help the situation.

When things don't go our way, we begin to ask two very dangerous questions. First, we start with the whys. In this scenario, whys would probably look something like this:

- Why didn't I prepare more for this presentation?

- Why was my boss looking at his phone?

- Why couldn't I say that one word correctly?

From an objective point of view, consider where these kinds of questions are leading you. These types of whys are pretty accusatory, and they don't inspire any further action on your part. (Other than feeling bad about yourself.) Moreover, none of these questions have clear answers, leading you even further down the path of harsh self-criticism. In short, this kind of "introspection" accomplishes absolutely nothing. This line of questioning will probably encourage rumination rather than true introspection.

Rumination, or cyclical negative thinking, when we reflect on past events, is perhaps the biggest enemy of true introspection. It's during rumination that we start to ask the second set of dangerous questions, which all typically begin with the words "I should have." All of a sudden, *Why didn't I prepare more for this presentation?* becomes *I should have prepared more for this presentation,* pulling us further into the cycle of self-loathing and self-pity.

Needless to say, none of this is constructive. As one of my university professors used to say, don't "should" on yourself! Instead of falling into endless whys and I should haves, it's far better to focus on whats. In other words, the main goal of introspection should be the objective description of facts.

One model for this is the BOOST (balanced, objective, observable, specific, and timely) model, which can help us stay on track when we engage in self-led introspection. If you're keeping a journal, it may benefit you to write a brief summary for each letter. Circling back to the example above, let's apply our BOOST model:

1. **Balanced**—I fumbled over my words a bit during the presentation. It was probably because I was feeling nervous. Everyone trips over their words sometimes. I'm sure it's not the weirdest thing someone's seen during a presentation! I prepared as best I could with the time I had. Any more time would have taken my energy away from other important work.

2. **Objective**—My boss was looking at his phone during my presentation. This could have been for several reasons, none of which I can presume to know! He may be dealing with a situation that I didn't know about, or he could have just needed a brain break.

3. **Observable**—While my delivery didn't go to plan, I still conveyed all of the information I wanted to get across to my audience. Even though I tripped over some of my words, I saw people taking notes about the information on my slides.

4. **Specific**—I fumbled my words a few times, but I mostly struggled with one or two terms in particular. In future presentations, I'll try to find easier synonyms for these terms.

The last BOOST metric, timely, refers to the amount of time that passes between the event in question and your BOOST analysis. Ideally, self-reflection should happen no sooner than a day and no later than a week from the event you're thinking about.

In addition to doing this kind of exercise yourself, it may also benefit you to loop in other relevant parties. For instance, if an interaction at work didn't go the way you planned, you might reach out to someone and politely request their help by completing a short BOOST analysis. While it might seem a bit corny or overly formal, getting a second opinion from someone you trust—like a boss, colleague, or friend—can help you minimize rumination and get a better handle on your external self-awareness.

Aside from frameworks like BOOST, there are a couple of other things you can work into your self-growth regimen to increase your self-awareness. This includes things like:

- identifying your strengths and weaknesses (Make sure to cite objective examples!)

- practicing mindfulness and meditation

- being genuinely curious about yourself, your behavior, and the people around you

- intentionally putting yourself into new and constructive situations (Think of a new class, project, or hobby.)

- trying to avoid comparing yourself to others on social media, especially platforms like Instagram

- setting daily check-in times to take stock of your day

- upping your "people time" by spending more time with friends, meeting new people, and deepening your existing relationships

All of these activities can give you a better sense of yourself and your standing with others, clarifying your decision-making process, and simplifying the pathway toward assertive communication.

Building Self-Esteem in the Context of Assertiveness

How do you eat a whale?

This may seem like a bizarre question, but eating a whale is oddly similar to the task you're currently facing. The truth is you can't acquire assertiveness overnight, the same way you can't eat a whale all at once. In the face of an immense task, your only option is to take small steps toward the finish line. Over time, these small steps compound into meaningful progress, scaffolding yesterday's knowledge and building a strong foundation.

In your quest for assertiveness, self-awareness is only one aspect of this foundation. Your next step is building your self-esteem. So, how *do* you eat a whale? One bite at a time.

Self-esteem is a crucial part of our self-image and is usually comprised of thoughts, opinions, and beliefs about ourselves. We then take these beliefs and overlay them onto whatever level of self-awareness we have. Paired with self-awareness, self-esteem (or lack thereof) is essentially ground zero in terms of how we see ourselves in the world. High self-awareness and high self-esteem generally result in well-adjusted, confident, and assertive people, while those with any kind of awareness and low self-esteem are generally less happy and less productive.

Make no mistake—self-esteem has wide-ranging effects that can make waves across all the different parts of your life. This includes areas like your:

- decision-making processes

- recognition of your strengths and weaknesses

- ability to learn and handle new situations

- time management skills

- social, professional, and academic success

The importance of self-esteem for long-term personal growth can't be overstated. That being said, researchers, psychologists, and mental health professionals have debated the benefits and consequences of self-esteem for decades, continually performing more research to explore (and sometimes disprove) our perceptions of self-esteem. According to some, our society has overstated the importance of self-esteem, while others believe that we haven't fully reckoned with the full effects that self-esteem has on mental health outcomes.

Due to the sheer size of the body of research on this topic, some scholars have resorted to things like literature reviews and meta-analyses (statistical analyses that draw and compile data from dozens of studies) to better understand the wider effects of self-esteem. According to one such meta-analysis from 2022, researchers found that the data supported the wide-ranging benefits that stem from having high self-esteem, despite apprehensions from other researchers and academics (Orth & Robins).

More specifically, the authors of this particular meta-analysis defined four different areas that were empirically observable as a direct result of high self-esteem:

- more satisfying personal relationships

- better outcomes at school and work

- improved mental and physical health

- prevention of antisocial behavior (such as violence)

These benefits held up across all ages, races, and genders. Moreover, Orth and Robins were able to isolate the many lifestyle variables that impact these areas of life. In other words, they proved that high self-esteem *caused* these benefits, rather than simply being a byproduct of other factors.

While studying high self-esteem and its benefits, Orth and Robins also discovered another fascinating thing. In their words (2022, p. 44):

> Both interpersonal and intrapersonal mechanisms might account for the adaptive effects of high self-esteem. For example, high self-esteem might facilitate initiating and maintaining social relationships, resulting in a stronger social network and greater availability of emotional, instrumental, and informational support, which may lead to positive outcomes in many life domains beyond relationships...High self-esteem also strengthens persistence after rejection and failure which again may lead to better outcomes.

Consider some of the vocabulary choices here: highly effective "interpersonal and intrapersonal mechanisms" sound a lot like what we might find in assertive communicators, right? From bouncing back from rejection to expressing yourself to others to building relationships across different areas of your life, it's clear that assertiveness and self-esteem are deeply connected.

Developing high self-esteem isn't easy, but it can certainly lead you closer to becoming an assertive communicator. Like self-awareness, building up your self-esteem is a process that takes time and effort, and perhaps even more personalization than other elements that contribute to assertiveness. To get you started, here are three things to work into your personal growth routine:

- Doing things you enjoy, like hobbies or volunteering.

- Focusing on the positive relationships in your life, and trying to put extra effort into the relationships that reinforce a positive self-image.

- "Chunking," or setting a manageable and achievable challenge for yourself such as learning a new recipe or reading a book.

Changing Your Mindset and Beliefs

In addition to becoming more self-aware and heightening your self-esteem, there's yet another factor that's integral to your path toward building assertiveness. Whether you're coming from a passive or aggressive communication style, the underlying issue that prevents you from embracing an honest and assertive way of communicating is the same. Somewhere underneath your behavior, you aren't being completely honest with yourself.

Let's explore what this means by looking at the concept of an *inner voice*, also sometimes called *self-talk*. Your inner voice is a term that encompasses all of the thoughts, opinions, and beliefs you hold about yourself while you're going about your life. These thoughts can take many different forms:

- running dialogue (or actual words that pop into your head)

- purposeful and conscious things you think about

- random thoughts directed at yourself

- images or memories that focus on one or more aspects of yourself

As we've seen through exploring self-awareness and self-esteem, your inner voice doesn't always line up with reality. The inner voice is the origin of the *whys* and *shoulds* that can bubble up after something goes wrong in our lives. The inner voice can also sometimes be the culprit when it comes to low self-esteem.

The presence of an inner voice is a relatively new research area in psychology. A team of cognitive scientists from the University of Copenhagen and the University of Wisconsin-Madison discovered that not everyone has an inner voice, a phenomenon they termed *anendophasia*. "It speaks to the surprising diversity of our subjective experiences," researcher Gary Lupyan told *Scientific American* (Makin, 2024, p. 2).

While our inner mental worlds can differ vastly, researchers also discovered that those with strong inner voices can't just switch off their inner dialogues. As a result, those with strong inner voices tend to have a heavier stream of inner dialogue in their waking hours (Makin, 2024).

For those with low self-esteem, this can be a truly terrible thing. With a non-stop inner dialogue that makes you feel bad about yourself, it's no wonder why gaining assertiveness can feel like a huge hurdle.

Luckily, there are several ways to minimize negative self-talk and start changing your underlying beliefs about yourself. The first step in this process is to monitor what your inner voice is saying as much as you can. Usually, negative self-talk begins with thinking traps like:

- idealizing perfection

- comparing yourself with others

- disqualifying positive experiences or traits you have

- fortune-telling, or preemptively expecting negative outcomes

- mind-reading, or assuming that others think the worst of you

- black-and-white thinking that leaves no room for nuance

- magnification of bad experiences or qualities

- jumping to conclusions

These traps can send you into a downward spiral that results in rumination, something that assertive communicators should try their best to avoid.

When you notice that your inner voice is veering towards any one of these thinking traps, try to figure out the cause of the negative self-talk. Was there a particular person or event that prompted it? Was there a situation that made you feel nervous? Whatever it is, make a mental note of the trigger for future reference.

When you catch yourself falling into thinking traps, you can use the ABC framework to stop the negative self-talk in its tracks. Created by psychotherapist Albert Ellis, the ABC framework is a simple, in-the-moment exercise that you can use to pull yourself out of the loop of negative self-talk. The ABC framework works like this:

1. **Activating event:** Identify the activating event, and try to be as specific as possible when you describe it.

2. **Belief:** Examine your knee-jerk emotional reaction to the event. What is your inner voice saying? What thinking traps could your inner voice be falling into? What is your biggest fear or anxiety surrounding the activating event?

3. **Consequence:** Consider the emotional consequences of your knee-jerk beliefs. Do they make you feel sad or angry? How strong are these feelings?

4. **Dispute:** This is where you begin to play Devil's Advocate. Instead of accepting your knee-jerk beliefs, interrogate them by asking questions or coming up with evidence to the contrary. As much as possible, try to provide yourself with observable evidence to support your arguments, and consider whether your original beliefs were logical or reasonable. Do your original beliefs serve you in any way? Do they help you reach your goals? Would a good friend believe the same things? Use your conclusions to develop new beliefs that are based on evidence and that help you reach your goals in some way.

5. **Effect:** With these new beliefs in tow, look at how you feel. How will these new beliefs impact your behavior going forward? Do they make you feel better than your original beliefs? How?

Even though you can't flip the metaphorical switch on your inner voice, you *can* change the things it says to you. Improving your inner monologue and stopping negative self-talk can deeply impact your future behavior and beliefs about yourself. With time, energy, and lots of practice, positive self-talk will soon become a habit that leads you to make better decisions, be more truthful to yourself, and help you communicate more assertively.

Adopting a Growth Mindset

If you've been active in the professional sphere any time over the last few years, you've likely heard the term "growth mindset" more times than you can count. But, outside of the corporate world, what exactly does that mean?

A *growth mindset* is the belief that abilities, intelligence, and talents can be developed and enhanced through dedication, effort, and learning. This concept contrasts with a *fixed mindset*, where individuals believe their attributes are static and unchangeable. The idea of a growth mindset, popularized by psychologist Carol Dweck, emphasizes that challenges and setbacks are opportunities for growth rather than insurmountable obstacles. Embracing this mindset fosters resilience, persistence, and a love of learning, which are crucial for personal and professional development.

Individuals with a growth mindset view failures as valuable feedback and a natural part of the learning process. Instead of being discouraged by mistakes, they analyze what went wrong, adjust their strategies, and try again with improved tactics. This perspective encourages continuous improvement and innovation. It also promotes a healthier attitude toward risk-taking, as people are more willing to step out of their comfort zones and explore new possibilities, knowing that their efforts will lead to growth over time.

By learning and practicing your sense of assertiveness, you'll likely begin to cultivate a growth mindset naturally. However, that doesn't mean you can't also make an effort to develop a growth mindset on your own. If you're leaning toward the latter option, here are a few things to get you started:

1. **Embrace Challenges:** Approach challenges as opportunities to learn and grow rather than obstacles to

overcome. Seek out tasks that push your boundaries and require effort. When faced with difficulties, remind yourself that setbacks are a natural part of the learning process and an opportunity to improve.

2. **Learn From Feedback:** View feedback, whether positive or constructive, as valuable information for growth. Instead of taking criticism personally, use it as a chance to identify areas for improvement and develop new skills. Actively seek feedback from others to gain different perspectives and insights. We'll discuss this more in-depth in later chapters.

3. **Persist in the Face of Adversity:** If there's one thing you take away from this book, it should be that persistence is the most valuable behavior you can adopt. Cultivate resilience by persisting through setbacks and failures. Develop a mindset that views challenges not as indicators of incompetence but as opportunities to strengthen your abilities. Practice perseverance and resilience by setting small, achievable goals and working steadily towards them.

4. **Adopt a Learning Mentality:** Embrace a lifelong learning mentality by staying curious and open to new experiences. Engage in activities that expand your knowledge and skills, whether through formal education, reading, or practical experiences. Seek out opportunities to acquire new skills and knowledge that align with your interests and goals.

5. **Surround Yourself With Growth-Minded Individuals:** Seek out mentors, peers, or colleagues who exhibit a growth mindset. Surrounding yourself with supportive individuals who encourage and challenge you can reinforce your own growth-oriented

beliefs and behaviors. Engage in discussions and collaborations that promote learning and development.

By consistently applying these strategies, you can gradually shift from a fixed mindset to a growth mindset, fostering a belief in your ability to learn, adapt, and achieve greater success in your life. In the next chapter, we'll discover how all of these factors—from a growth mindset to high self-esteem—can be accomplished using the power of words.

Chapter 4:

Developing Assertive

Communication Skills

With the mental foundation of self-awareness, self-esteem, and positive self-talk, it's time to start working away at our main goal: communicating assertively. You don't have to be an expert at positive self-talk, self-esteem, or self-awareness to start practicing assertiveness techniques. As always, assertiveness demands no prerequisites, and only requires that you're open to learning and trying new things out!

Before we get into the specifics of new assertive communication techniques, it's worth taking a realistic look at what to expect as you begin this new growth process. In all likelihood, things won't go exactly as planned when you make your first forays into assertive communication. You might not come across as you want to, or people might not react how you expect them to. This is perfectly normal, and it's no reason to give up your efforts. Before you get out there and start communicating assertively for the first time, remember these five things:

- **Don't be afraid.** I know what you're thinking—easy to say, hard to do in practice! Fear and anxiety are completely natural responses when you begin making big changes in your life. However, it's important to think of these changes (and yourself) in the context of something bigger. Chances are, all of the people you see every day are also trying out new things in their lives. No one is perfect; we're all trying to better ourselves. Even thinking about trying to improve yourself is a commendable endeavor!

- **Start small.** You don't have to change everything about your communication style overnight. This is not a healthy or sustainable way to improve yourself. Instead of jumping all in, think about what small, manageable pieces of assertiveness you can include in your next business meeting, school conference, or any other interaction.

- **Put in some face-to-face time.** All too often we try to make changes from the comfort of our own homes or behind our phone screens. While this is marginally helpful for some, it's also important to acclimate yourself to in-person interactions. In addition to making assertive communication easier, getting away from your keyboard will contextualize your efforts and build self-awareness.

- **Keep track of your efforts.** Even if you don't feel like you're making progress, it's important to measure what you're doing—what methods you've tried, what works or doesn't, and what situations you've succeeded in. This doesn't have to be anything fancy. Your phone's notes app will do just fine, or you could put pen to paper by using a physical notebook to journal for five minutes every day. Over time, this will help you see how far you've come.

- **Keep going.** It's tough to make big lifestyle changes, especially mental changes that require breaking persistent habits. Adopting assertiveness in your daily interactions won't happen overnight. While it's natural to be anxious for results, it's crucial to maintain momentum even when you don't succeed. Your future self will thank you!

With all of this in mind, let's now turn to some basic tips and tricks for becoming more assertive in your day-to-day life.

Verbal Communication

It's crucial to choose your words wisely. From your inner voice to the labels that society assigns to you, words have a deep impact on the way that you conduct yourself. Words are your best defense against falling into passivity or aggression. Even small changes and additions to your speech can make a huge difference when you're having tough conversations.

It's important to look at others through the same lens that you apply to yourself. In the context of assertive communication, you can use the same frameworks and tools we've already talked about. For one, the BOOST framework is a great tool when it comes to dealing with others. In the same way that you gauge yourself through evidence that's balanced, objective, observable, and specific, you need to give the same grace to others by being an honest, conscientious, and effective communicator.

You might recall this sentiment from Chapter 1, emphasized by psychologist Heidi Grant Halvorson—trying to guess what other people are thinking or feeling can get very old, very fast. Your first goal when being assertive is to remove some of the guesswork that other people have to do. You want what you say to accurately (but kindly) reflect what you think in a way that will get your message across properly if the other person were to apply the BOOST method.

Let's review a few hypotheticals to see how this might look in practice.

You're rushing to get ready for work one morning when your doorbell rings. It's one of your newer friends. They ask if you want to go to brunch at a new restaurant downtown. This clearly isn't urgent, but they're asking anyway even though they know your work schedule.

We always want to be there for people in our network, but your friend's request in this scenario isn't considerate or fair. An assertive communicator would take a few moments to process the situation to determine the best path forward, and then describe the situation from their point of view.

I'm excited to try that new restaurant too, but I'm feeling a little rushed right now. I would offer to drive you if I wasn't working today, but I have a project coming up and I can't take the day off. How about I send you my schedule for next week? That way, we can plan a brunch date. I really need to get going now, but it was great seeing you!

This type of response is measured and cordial, and it offers insight into what you're feeling and thinking. Rather than hemming and hawing like you might see in a passive approach, or exploding with frustration like you might see in an aggressive approach, this response gives the other person a chance to reassess their request based on where you're coming from.

In addition to staying firm but conscientious, this type of response also accomplishes three things. The first sentence allows you to establish common ground with your friend; that you also want to try the new restaurant. Secondly, this response suggests a possible solution—that your friend takes another look at your schedule and you plan a time that works for you both to meet. Finally, this reply lets you carve out time for this friend in the future by suggesting that you try out the restaurant together.

In short, assertive responses to situations like this allow for:

- honesty

- firmness but kindness

- a possible solution to a problem

- the potential to strengthen relationships and draw boundaries

There are a couple more things you might've noticed in the above example. For one, the response uses a lot of "I" statements. This is perhaps one of the best tools you can call upon when you're at a loss for what to say. Statements that begin with phrases like "I feel," "I wish," or "I want" are a great way to claim your emotions and express yourself. Doing this keeps the person you're speaking to from getting defensive. For instance, consider the difference between these two statements:

I feel a little annoyed that you expect me to take time off of work right now. I would appreciate it if you checked my schedule to see when I'm free.

You don't care about my life, and you don't listen to me when I ask you to do simple things.

The former uses "I" statements to take pressure off of the other person while still placing the onus for action on their shoulders. The latter, however, comes across as accusatory, and will likely inflame any tensions that exist in the relationship. If one were to use the second statement in this hypothetical, a friend knocking on your door might soon turn into an argument—or even worse, a burnt bridge. Strengthening relationships while still holding your ground is a key aspect of assertiveness, and "I" statements are an effective way to accomplish that.

In addition to using "I" statements whenever possible, there are several other simple mechanisms that can help you work toward building an assertive communication style.

- **Sticking to the facts and staying away from judgments.** This point aligns closely with the "O" of the BOOST method. Observable actions, words, or behaviors are far more likely to get you what you want when you're in the midst of a tough conversation. Things you know to be true, like your own feelings, past experiences, and previous conversations, are all great tools to call upon. Meanwhile, emotional judgments and moral grandstanding are both likely to make others feel defensive, in addition to being rather faulty evidence.

- **Avoiding quantifiers.** English speakers use quantifiers and degree words all the time in common speech. In fact, I just used one a few words ago! Words like "all," "very," "extremely," "always," and "never" are typically used to add a little extra to our everyday speech. However, they can work against us when we try to describe our thoughts or feelings. When you're trying to be assertive in conversation, it's best to stick to specific numbers or facts instead of hyperbole. For example, consider the difference between "You're always late, you don't care about our relationship at all!" and "This is the second time this week that you've been over 15 minutes late. Can we talk about that?"

- **Avoiding criticism.** Depending on what communication style you normally employ, it may feel natural to criticize yourself or the person you're speaking to. This is not constructive and can make difficult conversations worse. Instead of saying something like "I know I'm too emotional, but I really don't like the way you're always late," an assertive communicator would say "The fact that you're always late makes me feel sad and frustrated." In the same vein, an assertive communicator would replace "You have no manners!" with "I would like it if you respected my time more."

Finding the right words can be difficult, especially when you're in the midst of an uncomfortable conversation. Odds are that you won't always be able to find the perfect words to describe exactly how you feel all the time. Assertiveness is not, however, about being the most eloquent speaker in the room—it's about getting your point across in a firm, honest way. As you practice assertive communication, you'll find that describing your thoughts and feelings becomes easier over time.

Nonverbal Communication

Words aren't the only way to communicate our thoughts and feelings. In his 1971 book *Silent Messages*, psychologist and professor Albert Mehrabian first described his infamous 7-38-

55 rule, investigated through a brief experiment. The hypothesis of Mehrabian's experiment was this: 7% of meaning is communicated via words, 38% is communicated through one's tone of voice, and 55% is communicated via one's body language (Michail, 2020).

This has been disproven time and time again, and even Mehrabian went on to say that his findings were misinterpreted by the media and public (Lapakko, 2007). The idea that a whopping 93% of *all* human communication is nonverbal is perhaps a silly one, according to most psychologists and academics today. However, the conclusion of Mehrabian's 1971 experiment yielded decades of research and interest in the area of nonverbal communication.

Let's make one thing crystal clear—to communicate assertively, with clarity, and with conscientiousness, you absolutely need to use your words. There's no denying that words can communicate infinitely more nuanced meanings than your posture or tone does.

Keeping this in mind, nonverbal communication does play a role in how you come across. Let's revisit the example we looked at above.

I'm excited to try that new restaurant too, but I'm feeling a little rushed right now. I would offer to drive you if I wasn't working today, but I have a project coming up and I can't take the day off. How about I send you my schedule for next week? That way, we can plan a brunch date. I really need to get going now, but it was great seeing you!

Now, imagine that you delivered this response by yelling angrily with a frown on your face. This would seem a tad incongruous, wouldn't it? The words you're saying are communicative and conscientious, but your overall demeanor is aggressive and off-putting. If said with this kind of body language, your friend would probably run away from your house and never come back.

While maybe not as exaggerated as that example, we see the consequences of non-assertive body language every day. I've personally seen the effects that body language and delivery can have on your day-to-day interactions. As someone with a life-long RBF—otherwise known as a "resting b***h face"—I've always had to dedicate extra effort toward expressing myself in a way that reflects how I actually feel.

Several years ago, my RBF became glaringly apparent when I walked into a locally-owned coffee shop on my way to work. The veteran barista wasn't there, and in her place stood a new hire. Thinking nothing of it, I joined the line and began scrolling through my phone. As the line in front of me shrank and I stepped up to the counter, the new barista began to look a little worried as he recited the typical "Hi! What can I get started for you today?" That was when I realized I had been unintentionally frowning at my phone for the better part of five minutes. This wasn't because I was angry or frustrated; as I had learned over the years, my expression when I'm extremely focused can come off as being mad. As soon as I said "Hi!" and smiled, however, the worry vanished from the barista's face.

In times when we lack sufficient information from the person we're interacting with, we usually rely on context to make judgments about how to communicate in the future. In the case of the new barista at my local coffee shop, he probably thought he was going to have to deal with an angry customer, an over-complicated coffee order, or a $0 tip. This was not the case, but from a bird's-eye view, it's easy to see how we might extrapolate factors like body language and facial expressions onto the broader situation.

As we've said, you don't want to leave people hanging when it comes to communicating your thoughts and feelings. Instead of words (and sometimes even when we do provide context), our body language can tell a story that's completely different than how we actually feel.

Knowing this, it's important to keep these factors in mind when you're communicating assertively in tough conversations.

- **Keeping an open but commanding posture.** Ideally, your posture will communicate a clear message of strength and casualness. Try to avoid slouching or standing too rigidly.

- **Looking at the person you're talking to.** This may seem like a basic thing, but difficult, anxiety-inducing conversations can prompt us to deviate from the norm. Avoid looking at the floor, remember to keep your head up, and try to make eye contact with the person you're speaking to. When talking about eye contact, it's also important to know a little bit about the background of the people you're interacting with. In some cultures, lots of direct eye contact can be seen as offensive or aggressive, which is something you want to avoid. (In Chapter 7, we'll talk more about the role that multiculturalism and diversity play in developing an assertive communication style.)

- **Keeping your voice even.** Raising your voice is never advisable when you're having difficult conversations. Doing this will buy you a one-way ticket into an argument. On the flip side, speaking very softly or shyly won't communicate the kind of firmness that we aim to achieve in assertive communication. Instead, try to speak at a normal volume, with little emotional influence. Aside from volume, tone is another crucial aspect of how you deliver information. Tone, which includes things like voice pitching and sentence intonation, can convey a lot of information about how we're feeling. As a quick exercise, try standing in front of a mirror and saying the phrase "Sure, no problem" in a happy, amicable tone. Then, try to say the phrase in a standoffish, mean way. Then, try to seem bored or uninterested when you say the phrase. You'll note that with every iteration of the sentence, your voice changes to match your emotions, even though your emotions are hypothetical! With this in mind, it's crucial to avoid things like sarcasm or irony in your daily interactions. Similarly, try to not let your anxiety or feelings dictate what your tone of voice sounds like.

- **Maintaining a steady facial expression.** Sometimes, we don't even know we're making a face until someone calls it out! Before you jump into a difficult conversation, take a few moments to consider what your face is doing. Are you frowning? Are you smiling? If possible, try to find a comfortable baseline expression that you can maintain throughout the entirety of your conversation.

While all of the techniques and methods we've gone over in this chapter are great tools to get you started with communicating assertively, they're not the entire picture. You won't solve all of your communication woes by simply using "I" statements, and you probably won't resolve many of your interpersonal issues by just making eye contact. It would be wonderful to say that assertive communication is this easy, but it's usually not—again, a lifestyle shift as big as adopting assertiveness takes a lot of time, effort, and energy.

For many people, things like standing your ground, managing your emotional reactions, negotiating, and finding a middle ground are daunting. Yet, to properly incorporate assertiveness into your life, these kinds of hurdles are crucial to overcome. In the next chapter, we'll dive into some of the bigger, more intimidating tasks that assertiveness can help you overcome.

Chapter 5:

Techniques for Assertive

Interactions

On the surface, it may seem easy to be assertive in a conversation. Simply add a few choice words into your lexicon and bam! You'll get what you want out of every interaction. Unfortunately, this rarely happens.

We tend to oversimplify these things in our minds, playing out a specific conversation or interaction in our imaginations before we attempt them in real life. This kind of imaginary role-playing is common, especially among those with a preference for putting things into words. As said by English novelist Philip

Sington, "To rehearse imaginary conversations on paper is called literature. To do so aloud is called madness" (Killion, n.d., p. 1).

Many in society would likely agree with this sentiment, but imaginary role-playing is far from madness for those who feel anxious or nervous about a future event. You might remember cognitive scientist and researcher Gary Lupyan, whose findings we explored in Chapter 3. According to his team's research, imaginary role-playing before a stressful situation is a perfectly natural manifestation of our inner voice (Makin, 2024).

The problem arises when we try to apply our (usually flawed) imaginary role-playing practice to real-world interactions. Communicating with others isn't a math equation that gives you the chance to figure out all of the variables. When having difficult conversations or dealing with stressful situations, there's no way for you to know all of the variables in play. This dissonance between how you imagine your communication style and how your communication style actually goes over is perhaps one of the biggest culprits when it comes to miscommunication.

In this chapter, our goal is to minimize this dissonance by introducing a couple of methods that will bring you closer to true assertiveness, particularly in the face of some of the most difficult situations for new students of assertiveness. In addition to the tips and tricks we covered last chapter, these techniques will give you a baseline for what assertiveness should look like at work.

Saying "No" Without Guilt

In today's world, access is everything. Perhaps the most apt symbol of this is the smartphone, as well as the myriad gadgets and tech that we carry around with us every day. Our phones are effectively our portal to the modern world; the connection point that keeps us in the loop, informs us about current events, and impacts our chances of success. As a consequence, we essentially make ourselves accessible to everyone, all the time. This, we often believe, is in our best interests.

As more studies emerge, however, it has become clearer that giving the world access to us—and giving ourselves access to the world—via our phones has led to some nasty mental consequences. One such study examined the habits of 385 participants between the ages of 17 and 19 and found that adolescents who spent more time on their phones were more likely to develop anxiety and depression in adulthood (Coyne et. al., 2019).

Even more troubling is the fact that this didn't seem to be a temporary experience. For three years, researchers found that trends seen at the beginning of the study remained the same at the end of the research period. This isn't an isolated experience among Americans, either; similar results were found from studies all over the world, from Serbia (Višnjić et. al., 2018) to Saudi Arabia (Desouky & Abu-Zaid, 2020).

Already, we can see these results as a symbol of a larger trend; that is to say, giving the world unlimited access to our attention can make us feel worse. However, there is also international research that points to a more direct relationship between our smartphones and our communication styles. In South Korea, for example, one study found that out of 198 Korean university students, those who used their phones more were far more likely to have interpersonal issues in their lives. More specifically, the study looked at chronic social networking service (SNS) users. Shockingly, those who spent a lot of time on social media platforms were far less likely to have an assertive communication style (Gu et. al., 2016).

From a global perspective, there's ultimately nothing we can do about the prevalence of things like social media services or apps. This even extends to other areas of our lives, from career opportunities to dating apps. With such potent algorithms in our pockets virtually 24/7, it's no wonder that we have a hard time putting our phones down.

However, in the context of learning assertive behaviors, the ability to cut off others' access to your attention is essential. In short, you need to know how and when to say "no."

There's no denying that this is a difficult skill to learn. From staring at our phones to turning down requests in person, saying "no" can sometimes feel like the worst social faux pas you can make.

Just like with social media, saying "no" to in-person requests can trigger your sense of FOMO, or fear of missing out. What if the project you just rejected at work turned out to be a great opportunity? What if the party you just said "no" to turned out to be great? What if there was something you missed by declining that invitation? No matter the scenario, the what-ifs can begin to creep in and destroy your sense of self-esteem, making you feel unsure of your decisions and calling your judgment into doubt.

The first way you can begin digging yourself out of this hole is to recognize one of the biggest issues when it comes to our inability to deliver rejections. If you're active on social media or if you're interested in pop psychology, you might've already heard of *boundaries*. A boundary is a label used to describe the personal limits and guidelines that we can set for ourselves to protect our well-being and define how others can interact with us. They're essential for maintaining healthy relationships, ensuring respect, and preserving our mental, emotional, and physical health. One of the biggest culprits that we can point to when we feel uncomfortable saying "no" are weak boundaries.

Before we find our boundaries being pushed, there are some signs to watch out for, such as:

- feeling suddenly stressed or anxious

- noticing small changes in your day-to-day life

- ambiguous interactions that leave you wondering what you just discussed

- feeling more tired or run down than normal

Techniques for Saying "No"

All too often, we don't learn the art of saying "no" until we're already well into our adult lives. No one knows this better than lifestyle and psychology blogger Thendral Uthaman, who writes about her self-described quarter-life crisis and the subsequent areas of personal growth that she explores. In one post, she explains her perspective on learning to say "no" (Uthaman, 2024, p. 21):

> One of the things that blew my mind in my twenties was, "'No' is a complete sentence." Like, you're telling me I can just say "No"? And everything will be fine? here's something else I've realized: saying "no" doesn't make you a bad person. If anything, it just makes sure you offer the best version of yourself to the things and people that actually matter.

This realization comes as a shock to many, especially those who discover their ability to say "no" in empowering ways. As is usually the case when it comes to self-improvement, internet forums like Reddit and Quora are flooded with questions, advice, and anecdotes about how best to deliver rejections assertively.

In one such post from 2023, a forum participant explained his predicament. A chronic people pleaser, he found that his inability to say "no" was messing up all areas of his life. Another user with the handle trainmax responded with how he took his first baby steps in the realm of delivering rejections, writing (trainmax, 2023):

[I've] been the free IT-guy to fix or setup phones, computers, websites, or even TVs, first for my family...then for my friends...then for their friends. For. Years. [I] couldn't say no. THE trick that helped me was to say "Yes, I can do that. Next Friday, from 7:00pm until 8:00pm I have a free spot in my agenda. Just bring your stuff to my place." The answer usually was "oh, I don't have time then... " or "Oh, I thought you'd come to my place..." And that did it for me. It was now THEIR problem. I've even gained enough confidence from this to say "no" in other areas of my life now.

As with all other aspects of assertive behavior, the changes in your communication style don't have to take place overnight. If you're not entirely comfortable with saying "no" outright, you can take smaller and more manageable steps that allow you to approach your goals from a better vantage point. To get you started, however, consider these factors the next time you need to say "no:"

- Keep your "no" direct and clear.

- Offer alternatives or suggest a postponement.

- Be honest about where you're coming from.

- Show empathy for the other person's point of view. ("I know this is important to you, but I really don't have the time to go to this concert with you.")

- Practice in the mirror or roleplay beforehand.

- Avoid over-explaining yourself.

Handling Criticism and Feedback

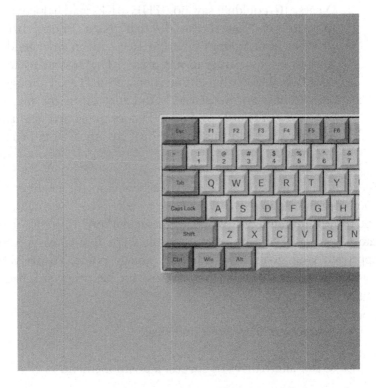

No matter where you are—at the office, in public, or at home with your romantic partner—criticism can be difficult to face. However, handling criticism and feedback effectively is crucial for personal and professional growth. Yet, we don't often see models for how to handle criticism effectively, leaving us to resort to whatever reaction comes first. This is not healthy, and it certainly doesn't qualify as assertive behavior!

To get a better sense of what we're looking for in these situations, we first need to understand the difference between being emotionally reactive and being emotionally proactive. *Reactive behavior* is behavior that hears criticism or feedback and then responds immediately with whatever emotion arises first.

We can think of this kind of behavior as similar to a sports fan whose team has just lost; based on immediate information, and resulting in immediate emotion. This isn't necessarily a bad thing, and you can't always mitigate the emotions that come up when you're confronted with information you don't like. However, assertive communicators typically favor proactive behavior or behavior that is forward-thinking. *Proactive behavior* revolves around possibilities that might happen in the future, watching for signs that things might go wrong, and developing courses of action to address these concerns. Emotionally proactive behavior relies largely on self-awareness and your ability to gauge the people around you. If their spouse seems more stressed than usual, for instance, a proactive person would take steps to mitigate potential stressors and help navigate the subsequent emotions.

While we can't see into the future, assertiveness necessitates proactive behavior. When receiving criticism, the proactiveness you demonstrate is effectively a manifestation of your assertiveness. It's imperative that you prioritize learning and growth over everything else. Don't view the criticism as a personal attack and don't let your emotions cloud your judgment. Try to provide potential solutions when possible.

When faced with criticism, don't:

- minimize the problem

- try to rationalize or justify

- make excuses for your mistakes

- try to sidestep the criticism

- shift the blame

Handling criticism hurts the most when it comes from people who are close to us. A new manager giving you pointers on a work project is one thing, but a piece of criticism from your spouse or close friend can sting. However, the same guidelines that you would apply in the office can (and should) be applied at home, particularly when it comes to listening to the people closest to you.

When we feel threatened or defensive in the face of criticism, it's easy for us to slip into an aggressive communication style. Writer, storyteller, and Quora advice columnist Andrew Weill writes about his evolving perspectives on personal growth and communication. Responding to a question about handling an overly defensive partner, Weill writes "My wife could have written this question, about 29 years ago. At that time, I was hugely defensive if criticized. I put the blame on my wife and convinced myself that the problem was all her" (Weill, 2023, p. 2).

In the face of raising three young children and dealing with chronic health issues, Weill was unintentionally letting his frustrations out on the people closest to him. When his wife suggested therapy and couple's counseling, Weill was skeptical (2023. p. 2):

> I went into this with the arrogant assumption that the counselors and workshop leaders would help straighten my wife out. I wasn't the problem person, no siree! Soon after, I learned that the way I was behaving actually interfered with achieving the level of intimacy I wanted. I needed to learn how to listen empathetically, without arguments, defenses, interruptions, or lectures. It was challenging work for me to really come to terms with some of my behaviors that were simply improper and at times hurtful...but we persevered, and the rewards have been magnificent.

If we look at this situation from the perspective of self-awareness, Weill's external self-awareness was greatly improved by listening to feedback and criticism, which in turn strengthened his relationship and improved his marriage.

At some point in your professional or personal life, you'll also probably find yourself on the flip side of this equation. Providing feedback may not be as daunting as receiving it, but it can still cause some anxiety when you're uncertain of how to say what's on your mind. To provide feedback without coming off as mean or judgmental, keep these things in mind:

1. **Focus on behavior and impact:** When giving feedback, concentrate on specific behaviors or actions rather than criticizing the person's character or personality. Describe the observable impact of their actions, both positive and negative, and how it affects the team or project.

2. **Be specific and descriptive:** Provide specific examples to illustrate your points. Use clear language and avoid vague or general statements. This helps the recipient understand exactly what they did well or where they can improve.

3. **Use the "feedback sandwich" approach:** Start with positive feedback or acknowledgment of strengths and efforts. Then, provide constructive criticism or areas for improvement. Finally, end on an encouraging note or with additional positive feedback. This approach balances criticism with recognition of strengths, making the feedback more palatable and motivating.

4. **Be timely:** Offer feedback as close to the observed behavior as possible. This ensures that the details are fresh in everyone's mind and allows the recipient to reflect on their actions promptly.

5. **Focus on Improvement and solutions:** Offer suggestions or recommendations for improvement rather than just pointing out flaws. Collaborate on creating actionable steps or goals for the future. Encourage the recipient to develop their, solutions, fostering ownership and commitment to change.

6. Maintain a positive and supportive **tone:** Use language that is constructive, respectful, and non-judgmental. Avoid using accusatory or harsh language that may escalate defensiveness. Aim to build trust and rapport, creating a safe environment for open communication.

7. **Follow up:** Check in periodically to see how the individual is progressing and offer additional support or guidance as needed. Recognize improvements and celebrate successes to reinforce positive behaviors.

Negotiation and Compromise

All too often, we look at negotiation and compromise as synonyms for conflict. As a consequence, our behaviors in situations that require negotiation and compromise are pretty revealing of our beliefs, our awareness, and our behaviors. This can bring out unsavory behaviors like defensiveness and anger, and it won't usually get you what you want.

Let's take a look at a hypothetical example to see how this might play out:

Two colleagues, Sarah and James, are assigned to work together on a critical project for their company. Sarah, known for her assertive communication style, believes strongly in taking a proactive approach and implementing innovative ideas to propel the project forward. James, however, prefers a cautious and methodical approach, prioritizing thorough analysis and risk assessment before making decisions.

As they begin working together, Sarah and James quickly encounter disagreements about how to proceed. Sarah advocates for rapid implementation of new technologies and strategies she believes will streamline processes and increase efficiency. She feels frustrated when James consistently raises concerns about potential risks and challenges, viewing his approach as overly cautious and resistant to change.

On the other hand, James becomes increasingly wary of Sarah's proposals, feeling that she dismisses his input and rushes into decisions without fully considering the implications. He believes her eagerness to innovate overlooks crucial details and potential pitfalls that could jeopardize the project's success.

As discussions escalate, both Sarah and James dig in their heels, focusing more on defending their positions rather than seeking common ground. They become entrenched in their respective viewpoints, leading to tension and a communication breakdown.

This lack of effective negotiation prevents them from reaching a compromise that integrates both innovative ideas and risk management strategies. Consequently, the project encounters delays and setbacks as Sarah and James struggle to move forward together. Their inability to negotiate effectively results in missed deadlines, confusion among team members, and increased stress levels. The project's progress is hindered, and morale within the team diminishes as frustrations mount.

The above scenario is the opposite of what good negotiations try to accomplish. In reality, negotiation and compromise should be conversations rather than arguments. Negotiating assertively involves clearly expressing your needs while respecting the other party's perspective.

To begin, thorough preparation is essential. Research all relevant information and define your goals, including what you're willing to compromise on. During the negotiation, communicate clearly by using "I" statements to express your thoughts and feelings without blaming others. Be specific about what you want, and stay calm and composed, even if the discussion becomes tense. If needed, suggest taking a short break to regroup.

Active listening is crucial. Show empathy by acknowledging the other person's perspective and asking them questions to clarify their position. Set clear boundaries and know your limits. Be firm but polite in expressing them. Focus on interests rather than positions to identify underlying needs and seek mutual gain. Positive body language, such as maintaining eye contact and an open posture, helps convey confidence and honesty.

Be prepared to walk away if your minimum needs are not met, understanding your best alternative to a negotiated agreement. Practice patience, take your time, and be prepared for multiple rounds of discussion if necessary. Aim for win-win solutions by collaborating with the other party and thinking creatively to find mutually beneficial outcomes. By using these strategies, you can negotiate assertively, ensuring your needs are met while maintaining respect and professionalism.

Knowing this, let's take a look at Sarah and James' situation if they had used assertive communication and proper negotiation techniques:

Initially, Sarah and James recognize their differing perspectives and the potential for friction. Rather than dismissing each other's viewpoints, they decide to approach their discussions with a commitment to effective negotiation and collaboration.

To begin, Sarah starts by outlining her vision for the project, emphasizing the benefits of implementing new technologies and strategies. She acknowledges James's concerns about risks and invites him to share specific areas where he foresees potential challenges. James responds by articulating his concerns in detail, providing evidence-based arguments to support his cautious approach. He acknowledges Sarah's innovative ideas and suggests ways to incorporate them while addressing the identified risks.

As the negotiation progresses, Sarah and James actively listen to each other's perspectives and seek common ground. They engage in constructive dialogue, brainstorming solutions that integrate both innovation and risk management. Sarah proposes phased implementation of new technologies, allowing for incremental adjustments based on James's risk assessments. James, in turn, supports Sarah's innovative initiatives with additional safeguards and contingency plans.

Throughout their negotiations, Sarah and James maintain open communication and mutual respect. They leverage their complementary strengths—Sarah's creativity and James's analytical rigor—to develop a comprehensive project plan that balances innovation with risk mitigation.

As a result of their effective negotiation, Sarah and James gain buy-in from key stakeholders and secure the necessary resources for their project. Their collaborative approach fosters a sense of unity among team members, who feel empowered to contribute to the project's success.

Ultimately, Sarah and James' ability to negotiate effectively leads to a well-executed project that meets objectives, exceeds expectations, and enhances their reputation within the company. Their example of constructive negotiation sets a precedent for future collaborations, promoting a culture of teamwork and innovation across the organization.

It's clear to see that assertiveness is absolutely crucial for effective negotiation and compromise. Summarizing everyone's thoughts, working together rather than competing, and fostering an environment of mutual respect can do wonders in getting you what you want.

As with everything in life, however, context matters. The same is true for assertiveness, especially as it becomes a lifelong skill. In the next chapter, we'll explore some of the different situations in which assertiveness comes into play, from workplace negotiations like the one above to social interactions that build personal relationships.

Chapter 6:

Assertiveness in Different

Contexts

As you might've already noticed, assertiveness isn't limited to one aspect of our lives. As a lifestyle tool and lifelong skill, assertive communication is something that can be applied to all areas of your life, from social gatherings to marriages to workplaces. This can be exceedingly difficult for some people, especially because we often adjust our personalities, behaviors, and tendencies (sometimes drastically) depending on what situation we find ourselves in.

Psychologists and researchers have identified two main personas that most people have: a professional persona and a personal one (Garone, 2017). This can be beneficial at times, particularly for those who want to keep a thicker layer of separation between their work lives and their home lives. A prison guard, for instance, will probably act very differently at home than they do at work.

However, this phenomenon can be seen across all sectors of the professional world, from doctors to corporate workers. For many, acting differently than they normally do is an inherent part of what it means to be at work. According to Cambridge researcher Sanna Balsari-Palsule, "We are so used to acting out of character for the sake of professionalism" that we often don't even know that we're doing it (Garone, 2017). This phenomenon has been coined "free-trait behavior," which basically describes our willingness to change our behaviors, personalities, and other traits to achieve things that we really care about.

Refinery29 writer Olivia Harrison experienced this firsthand during the COVID-19 pandemic, during which time her boyfriend started working from home. She had previously known him as a goofy, silly person who put on voices to amuse the couple's two cats; someone who would dance just to dance. When she heard his work persona for the first time, Harrison was stunned (Harrison, 2021, p. 2):

> It's been jarring to have a new sound ringing through our home over the last 13 months: work-voice. Every weekday, as I sit at my desk, typing away, I hear my boyfriend's deep voice, several octaves lower than the one he uses to serenade me and the cats...What work-voice has in common with our regular voices is that it too is nonsense, but it's a notably different type of nonsense than the kind we spew at one another for pleasure.

In the effort to keep our work and home lives separate, we often forego the standards or unspoken rules that accompany one or the other. This is the point at which assertiveness tends to get lost in the mix-up between our work and personal lives. As with many of the traits and behaviors we use in the different areas of our day-to-day lives, we may not even notice that our communication style changes when we step into different environments.

If you're anything like me, you might've used to view assertiveness as a formal way of communicating. I had no problem communicating assertively in the workplace and my academic career, but this style of communication would almost entirely dissolve when I stepped into social or personal contexts. If you aren't used to it, speaking directly and assertively to a spouse, close friend, or family member can feel a bit strange. Without the inside jokes, sarcasm, or fluff that marked so many of my relationships, it almost felt like I was distancing myself from the people I cared about most.

This, of course, was not the case. Assertiveness, if practiced correctly, doesn't weaken the relationships in your life or put distance between yourself and your loved ones. Assertiveness strengthens your personal, social, and professional lives by defining boundaries, expressing yourself more fully, and being more honest with the people you care about. Assertiveness isn't a solely formal tool; on the contrary, assertive communication is a life skill that should carry over to *all* the people you interact with.

In Personal Relationships

According to researchers Courtney Wright and Michael Roloff, neglecting assertiveness in your personal relationships is perhaps one of the worst things to do. In their research, published in *Communication Research Reports*, they write: "Some people believe that intimate partners should be able to understand each other's needs and feelings without their having to express them. Those holding 'mind reading expectations' often have less satisfying relationships" (Travers, 2023, p. 7). The same holds true, they found, in the other relationships in our lives.

Assertive communication in personal relationships involves expressing your thoughts, feelings and needs openly and honestly while respecting the rights and feelings of others. It fosters mutual respect and understanding, enabling both parties to communicate effectively without resorting to passive or aggressive behaviors. This type of communication allows you to set clear boundaries, share your true feelings, and address issues directly without fear of conflict.

By being assertive, you can resolve misunderstandings, prevent resentment, and build stronger, healthier relationships based on trust and transparency. When both parties are clear about their expectations and feelings, it reduces the likelihood of miscommunication and unresolved tensions. Assertive communication also helps in addressing issues as they arise, rather than letting them fester and potentially harm the relationship over time.

Additionally, assertive communication encourages empathy. When you communicate assertively, you not only express your own needs but also make space for the other person to share their perspective. This creates a more supportive and cooperative environment where both individuals feel valued and heard. In such an environment, both parties are more likely to work together to find solutions that satisfy both of their needs, leading to more harmonious and fulfilling relationships.

Assertiveness and Active Listening in Personal Relationships

Perhaps the biggest benefit of using assertiveness in your personal relationships is the act of listening. Sometimes we hear what our friends, family members, or partners are saying, but we aren't really listening. It's this distinction between hearing and listening that's given rise to the term "active listening," or our efforts to fully concentrate, understand, respond, and remember what others say to us. Active listening requires that you set aside all other distractions and use your body language to indicate to the other person that you're aware of what they're saying.

Active listening holds immense value, especially when communicating with someone close to you. It goes beyond simply hearing words; it involves fully engaging with the speaker, understanding their message, and responding thoughtfully. In personal relationships, active listening fosters a deeper connection and trust, showing that you value and respect the other person's thoughts and feelings.

According to Caitlyn Rogers and Lisa Schainker, assistant professors at Utah State University, active listening techniques have been proven to help your loved ones feel more comfortable sharing with you, build trust, and strengthen the security of the relationship (Rogers & Schainker, n.d.). By giving your full attention and demonstrating empathy, you create a safe space where open and honest communication can flourish.

In addition to all of the other assertiveness techniques we've covered so far, think about incorporating some of these active listening tips into your assertive communication style:

- Don't just wait for the other person to stop talking, and don't try to figure out what you want to say next before they're finished.

- Make eye contact and maintain a good posture that's oriented toward the person.

- Use other physical cues like nodding to indicate that you understand.

- Check for understanding once you're done by paraphrasing what the other person has said.

- Keep your assumptions, biases, and opinions in check when having tough conversations.

- Ask questions to cultivate a genuine interest in what the other person is expressing.

In the Workplace

When you're at work, your communication style can have significant and immediate effects on your professional life. Let's examine a brief example to see what this can look like:

Imagine that your boss has assigned a new project to you and one of your colleagues. The project isn't particularly difficult or crucial, but it does have a tight turnaround. You reach out to your colleague to schedule a time to collaborate, but they give you a vague answer by saying they'll check their calendar at a later time. This happens several times, and you're worried that you won't have enough time to finish the project.

At this point, you probably know how different communication styles would respond to this dilemma: the passive communicator would end up avoiding confrontation and doing all the work themselves, the aggressive communicator would become angry and start a direct conflict, and the assertive communicator would look for solutions while remaining firm about the project's timeline.

With this in mind, let's think about a slightly different scene. Instead of a colleague, picture that you need to complete this project with your boss. Your boss does the same thing that your colleague did in the first scenario: shirks their responsibilities, puts off the project, and gives you vague answers without any clear path forward. How would you approach them? Would you communicate with your boss differently than you would with your colleague? Would your attitude towards communication change?

As we've learned, assertiveness isn't typically limited to straightforward situations like the first scenario that we outlined above. In the workplace specifically, you'll also have to practice assertiveness with your bosses, colleagues, and everyone else you interact with. This can be tricky to navigate, especially when your professional reputation is on the line.

Communicating With Colleagues, Bosses, and Direct Reports

To make sense of some of the pressures that come with communicating assertively at work, we first need to take a look at how to best communicate with those of different positions than you. While the professional landscape has changed somewhat over the last few years, there's one thing that has remained the same: workplace hierarchies. There are various ways that employers can organize their authority levels, but the most common organizational structure is a hierarchical one.

To communicate effectively, you have to acknowledge both the context of the interaction as well as the role of the person you're speaking with. While you don't necessarily have to be prim and proper all the time, it's important to remember that the people you work with aren't usually your friends; adjusting your communication methods to reflect this is crucial.

At the most basic level, word choice and lexicon can immediately give people an insight into your sense of professionalism. In Chapter 4, we talked about some techniques you can use to improve your assertiveness on a verbal level, such as avoiding quantifiers, keeping criticism out of your responses, and managing your emotions. All of these things apply to assertiveness in the workplace, but there is an additional layer of lexical assertiveness that you can use to improve the quality of your interactions at work.

- **Avoid "I think" statements.** Consider the sentence "I think Plan A might be our best option." At first glance, nothing seems wrong with the sentence, right? Now, compare it with this sentence: "I'm confident that Plan A will yield the best results." When we're not sure about how our opinions will be received, we often revert to using "I think" as a buffer. If your middle school English teachers were anything like mine, you were probably taught time and time again that the words "I think" have no place in a persuasive essay. Aside from being redundant, the choice of verb doesn't inspire confidence from your audience. Thinking can be easily changed or swayed by emotions, and many of the things we think are malleable. The "I think" sentence in the above example also uses the word "might," which essentially doubles down on the sense of doubt the sentence conveys. By removing the weaker terms and replacing them with more assertive words like "confident" and "will," the speaker conveys a sense of certainty and conviction to their audience.

- **Rely on good old-fashioned politeness.** If you're anything like me, you often want to soften your vocabulary to make yourself seem more approachable. This is even more prevalent in the workplace, especially when speaking to colleagues or direct reports. While making yourself more approachable in the professional sphere isn't necessarily wrong, there *is* something wrong with softening your vernacular at the expense of your assertiveness at work. Personally, my former fatal flaw in this area comes in the form of two words: no problem. "No problem" is typically used after a "thank you" or in place of "you're welcome," a switch that's prevalent among younger generations. However, the phrase "no problem" inadvertently implies that the action you're being thanked for *could have* been perceived as a problem for you. The difference in meanings between "no problem" and "thank you" is subtle, but it's there. We make these kinds of replacements all the time, using phrases like "of course," "sure thing," and even "it's okay." Instead of trying to make yourself more approachable with these responses, opt for more traditional phrases that will reaffirm your assertiveness. Sometimes, a simple "you're welcome" can work wonders!

- **Replace coulds and shoulds with future-based suggestions.** When we feel frustrated or angry with someone at work, especially colleagues and direct reports, it's easy to bust out the "coulds" and "shoulds." It's reflexive to say something like "You could have started on this project earlier" or "You should manage your time better," but these sentiments are rarely productive. Imagine a colleague or boss used a "could" or "should" with you; you'd feel like they were blaming you for something, right? As an assertive communicator, your job is not to point fingers. Instead, try making future-based suggestions when you feel frustrated. Rather than "You could have started on this project earlier," opt for "In the future, I'd like you to periodically update me on your progress so we can make sure this doesn't happen again."

- **Minimize filler words and sounds.** All too often, filler words take up space in our verbal communications. If you're a social media native, you might've stumbled across the niche video genre of filler-word compilations. These videos take out all of the content words—words that convey an actual meaning—and leave only the filler words and sounds. Imagine for a moment that you're able to snap your fingers and apply this process to yourself. How many filler words would your video have? What would the ratio of filler words to content words be? As difficult of a habit as it is to kick, using meaningless words eats into our ability to communicate assertively. After all, if 40% of what you say is meaningless, then why would anyone listen to you? As much as possible, try to avoid words and sounds like "I mean," "actually," "well," "you know," "okay," "I guess," "yeah," and "um."

In addition to these lexical adjustments, there are other considerations to take into account when you interact with bosses. As always, the hierarchical structure of most workplaces requires you to acknowledge the station of the person you're interacting with. This is particularly important for interactions with bosses. Demonstrating a level of respect and professionalism is crucial for maintaining effective communication.

- **Stay away from slang, unnecessary jargon, and pop culture references.** Concerning our professional growth, we often want our bosses to like us. To this end, some people try to use slang, pop culture references, and jargon to encourage conversations with leaders. While wanting to improve your professional relationship with your leadership team is a great goal, chatting about your favorite TV show is not an effective way to demonstrate your professional competence. Casual conversation every once in a while won't necessarily hurt you but try to keep your relationships in the workplace professional.

- **Avoid categorical black-and-white statements.** When an immediate superior asks you to do something that you're unable to do, you might consider responding with something like "I can't help with that" or "That's impossible." These responses are firm, clear, and possibly effective; and they might even be mistaken for being assertive. However, assertiveness is a method of effective communication above all else. These responses are pessimistic, and they won't encourage your leaders to view you in a positive light. Eroding your professional relationships in this way does not constitute effective communication or assertiveness! When your plate is already full or when deadlines loom, try saying something closer to "Let's discuss what's possible in this situation" or "What I can do is..."

- **Use tag questions sparingly.** When speaking with people we often relegate ourselves to the position of "inferior." Instead of communicating our beliefs clearly and confidently, we turn our thoughts into questions. Statements like "We should go with Plan A" become "Plan A seems nice, doesn't it?" and the emphasis slowly moves towards seeking validation rather than saying what you believe. If seeking validation from your boss is your only goal in an interaction, then using phrases like "If it's okay with you" and "Don't you think?" is the perfect way to accomplish this. In the majority of workplace interactions, however, your goal should not be to seek validation. Chances are, your leaders value an assertive communicator rather than a "yes-man." Instead of ending your thoughts with sentence tags or questions, plainly state what you want to say and let them come to their own conclusions about whether or not they agree with you.

Handling Workplace Conflicts

Unfortunately, the miscommunications that we see in our personal and social lives can extend into the professional sphere. When people are passionate about what they do, or when pressures begin to rise, conflicts are bound to happen. As an assertive communicator, it's your responsibility to work through professional conflicts, even when it feels uncomfortable.

If you were previously a more passive communicator, then you're probably somewhat anxious about the idea of a conflict or argument at work. This anxiety has been studied by psychologists and mental health experts for decades, and the labels attached to it vary. In the context of your professional life, some experts posit that one's fear of conflict can lead to missed opportunities, particularly when it comes to zero-sum situations; situations in which your gains come at the expense of someone else's (Davidai et. al., 2022). This aligns almost perfectly with our definition of a passive communication style, considering that fear of conflict in zero-sum games requires one to rank their needs against others.

Another way to see this issue is from the perspective of confrontation. For some, confrontation in the workplace is synonymous with fighting. This results in negative outcomes like demotions, fraught professional relationships, and subpar products.

To overcome this, we need to dispel the notion that all conflicts entail strong negative emotions. In other words, conflict doesn't have to make you feel angry, afraid, or sad. Further, it's important to realize that these emotions don't necessarily predicate a conflict.

We should also dispel the idea that all conflicts are bad. In reality, professional conflicts can result in better work outcomes, stronger team dynamics, and a clearer sense of self-awareness in the workplace. From this perspective, conflict can actually be a beneficial factor in your professional life!

Understanding these ideas is the first step in managing the anxieties and fears that surround conflicts. Effective conflicts aren't fights. Rather, we can think of conflict as a heightened state of communication between parties.

The effectiveness of conflicts can vary depending on many factors. You can imagine how assertiveness contributes to healthier conflict, though. In addition to some of the assertiveness techniques we've discussed so far, workplace conflicts can also benefit from the following.

- **Managing emotions.** One of the biggest things that separates an unhealthy conflict from a healthy one is emotion. Unmitigated negative emotions can result in screaming matches, poor communication between parties, and damaged professional relationships. In the face of disagreement at work, it's crucial to manage your emotions. In practice, this looks like (a) defining what you want out of the conflict, how you feel about the issue at hand, and how you feel about the parties you're interacting with, and (b) taking time away from the situation when needed. While you can't manage others' emotions, you can do your part to keep tensions low and communication levels high.

- **Creating an elevator pitch for your ideas.** We often enter into conflicts without fully examining our plans, ideas, or needs. Conflicts that require you to explain yourself can make you feel defensive, resulting in frayed nerves. When you feel a conflict brewing, take a look at your perspective and try to interrogate the specifics of what you want. This means defining specific outcomes, providing reasoning, and expressing your ideas methodically and logically. To do this, consider creating a mini elevator pitch, or a 30-60-second presentation detailing the gist of your perspectives.

- **Looking for sustainable solutions rather than easy wins.** When conflicts turn into fights, parties usually look for wins wherever they can find them. This turns the interaction into a zero-sum game, with one party "winning" and the other party "losing." At work, zero-sum thinking can hurt everyone, especially when parties are in the same department or area. Instead of trying to win, try to contextualize conflicts by thinking of the health of your team—even when you disagree with team members. This mindset will strengthen your professional relationships and improve the outcomes of the conflict.

- **Summarizing others' ideas.** High-tension situations are rife with miscommunications. We tend to forget that others can't read our minds. An easy way to streamline conflict and minimize miscommunications is to briefly summarize other people's ideas in your own words. This doesn't have to be a long, drawn-out process; a simple phrase like "Let me make sure I understand..." or "To clarify..." can help you get a better sense of what people are *actually* saying.

- **Giving praise when needed.** Think about the last big fight you had with someone. At any point in the interaction did either party offer genuine praise? Probably not. Because fights entail winners and losers, we usually don't want to give the other party any wiggle room to win. As we've established, workplace conflicts are not fights; rather than individuals, *the team* either wins or loses. Given that you're essentially working with a team to solve a problem, giving praise when possible is a great way to show goodwill and strengthen relationships. This can be accomplished by throwing in simple phrases like "I like what you said before about XYZ" and "I respect how much you care about this issue." Doing this can go a long way in making a conflict more productive.

While it might sound strange, it may benefit you to plan these steps out before conflicts arise. Writing down a few key phrases, practicing de-escalation techniques in the mirror, and taking a few minutes to gauge your mental state before heading to work are great ways to ensure you're prepared to handle conflict.

For Women and People of Color in the Professional Sphere

If you're a woman or a person of color, chances are that developing assertiveness is more challenging for you. According to decades of research, social scientists have found that the way we perceive assertiveness varies drastically depending on race and sex. For starters, White women are seen in a far more negative light than White men when they express emotions at work, and they're far more likely to be labeled as "emotional" when they attempt to employ assertiveness techniques (McCormick-Huhn & Shields, 2021).

This was the case for a 29-year-old international marketing professional, who discovered one day that her male colleagues were not being held to the same standard as she was. In an interview with the Allbright Collective, she describes her experience (Selby, 2021, p. 7):

> When I was first called aggressive by a client in a meeting, I felt really guilty that I'd perhaps made someone feel bad. That was not my intention at all." But Lara later became incensed when she discovered male colleagues weren't being pulled up for using the same tone in their communications. I had to adjust my emails to include emojis and soften my language to appear more friendly," she says. "The downside to this was that often work didn't get completed the way I wanted or wasn't prioritized. I found it really hard to be assertive without being direct.

The severity of stereotyping grows worse when we consider the attitudes and biases that exist against Black and Brown bodies in the workplace. In one 2016 exploration, *Guardian* writer Rose Hackman described her sudden awareness of racial stereotyping when she and her Black family friend Justin traveled to Dearborn Heights, Michigan. As she investigated the racially motivated murder of 19-year-old Renisha McBride in the area, Hackman began to better understand the dangers that people of color face, even in the context of professional pursuits. As she writes (Hackman, 2016, p. 10):

> In America, black men have historically been depicted as aggressive, hypersexual and violent – to be controlled, to be exploited, to be tamed. The result of that construct and the accompanying racist fear and forced subjugation it justifies has been counterintuitive: black men in America are in fact...constantly at risk.

Even in his work in association with *The Guardian*, one of the most well-known newspapers in the nation, Justin still bore the burden of being perceived as angry or violent at the smallest move.

Perhaps the most at-risk group in the context of assertiveness is Black women. As we've seen time and time again, Black women are often the victim of immediate labeling in the workplace and the broader world. One exploration published in the *Harvard Business Review* (Motro et. al., 2022) explores the commonly-used descriptor for this kind of stereotyping: the "Angry Black Woman" label. From Justice Ketanji Brown Jackson to famous tennis star Serena Williams, Black women and women of color are consistently chastised for being angry even when the same actions from a White man would be considered assertive.

Knowing this, it's clear that not everyone who adopts assertiveness will be perceived in the same way. Although a growing number of organizations have implemented diversity, equity, and inclusion (DEI) initiatives aimed at incentivizing the onboarding of marginalized communities, the broader culture of race and sex still holds many back from embracing their assertiveness.

Opinions about potential solutions to this plague of biases and stereotyping vary. Some believe that marginalized groups should simply act with the same style of assertiveness common among White male professionals. Others believe that marginalized communities should be more careful when using assertiveness in the workplace.

While there's no clear-cut answer or blanket solution, it's obvious that personal safety should be your number one priority. If you feel that your safety is in danger, your first step should be to remove yourself from the situation. Barring unsafe situations, assertiveness remains a life skill that everyone can benefit from. For women, people of color, and other marginalized groups, however, some additional precautions can help you combat stereotyping in the workplace.

- Getting everything in writing, from emails to messages to all other communiqué that you receive from colleagues, direct reports, and bosses.

- Ensuring that you take care of your mental health outside of work, and taking the proper steps to protect your well-being.

- Reporting instances of stereotyping, unfair treatment, or racial/gendered preference to your company's HR department immediately. (And getting receipts at every possible point along the way.)

- Normalizing talking about stereotyping, biases, and microaggressions.

Workplace discrimination is completely contrary to assertiveness and promotes ideas that ultimately harm everyone in the workplace. There are many terms for this, but we can sum this idea up in the phrase "macho culture." This is a phrase that's typically associated with unhelpful and antiquated ideas about masculinity. This standard involves the prioritization of dominance, aggression, and winning at all costs, usually at the expense of others. Needless to say, being "macho" does more harm than good.

If you identify as a member of a majority group, whether it's a religious, ethnic, or gender majority, it's crucial that you do your part to combat discriminatory standards by sticking up for marginalized coworkers. Moreover, you can also fight "macho culture" by demonstrating the empathetic, compassionate, and highly communicative elements of assertiveness that we've learned about.

In Social Situations

Circumstances we don't often think about in the context of assertiveness are social situations. In some ways, practicing assertiveness in a social context is far more daunting than practicing assertiveness in the workplace or at home. This is because social situations are themselves more daunting than one's workplace or home.

According to one estimate from the National Institute of Mental Health in partnership with the Anxiety & Depression Association of America (ADAA), a whopping 15 million adults are clinically diagnosed with some level of social anxiety, making up about 7.1% of the U.S. population (National Institute of Mental Health, 2017). This figure is already astonishing enough, but it only accounts for those who receive a medical diagnosis. Given that not everyone in the U.S. is going to therapy, this number is likely higher than the current reports.

In situations where you're among a group of people, it can feel like you have to perform the most amicable, funniest, and most successful version of yourself. The pressure to be the best version of yourself can lead you to weaken your boundaries or forego your typical communication style. In short, assertiveness flies right out of the window.

However, assertiveness can take many forms. Unlike the things we often tell ourselves when we're faced with new and sometimes scary social situations, assertiveness doesn't require us to be the best. In the same way that active listening is an aspect of assertiveness that we don't often think about, other parts of assertive communication can suit us in social situations.

One aspect of assertive communication in social settings is the ability to assert boundaries effectively. This means communicating what is acceptable or not to you politely and firmly. For example, assertively declining invitations or requests that you are not comfortable with or expressing your discomfort if someone crosses a personal boundary demonstrates self-respect and encourages others to respect your boundaries, as well.

Additionally, assertive communication fosters genuine and open interactions with others. It encourages active listening, empathy, and mutual understanding. By expressing yourself assertively, you invite others to share their thoughts and feelings honestly, leading to deeper connections and more meaningful relationships.

Assertive individuals in social situations often find it easier to navigate social dynamics, handle conflicts gracefully, and build rapport with others based on honesty and mutual respect. Overall, assertive communication enhances social interactions by promoting authenticity, clarity, and mutual respect among individuals.

In addition to practicing the assertiveness techniques we've been discussing, there are many other steps you can take to minimize the social anxiety you feel.

- Attending therapy, specifically cognitive behavioral therapy and exposure therapy.

- Practicing mindfulness and meditation.

- Performing positive visualization techniques.

- Using deep breathing exercises before heading into social situations.

- Exercising regularly and eating a balanced, healthy diet.

- Spending time with family, friends, and other supportive figures in your life.

- Joining support groups.

- Journaling about your thoughts for a few minutes every day.

- Setting realistic goals based on the SMART framework.

All in all, taking care of your physical and mental health will build a strong foundation that you can rely on when you begin to feel anxious in social situations. In turn, these things will help you feel more confident as you adopt assertive communication techniques into your everyday life. In the next chapter, we'll talk more about barriers to assertiveness, as well as some methods for staying consistent.

Chapter 7:

Overcoming Barriers to

Assertiveness

Imagine that your boss assigns you a massive project, full of intricate details and lots of moving parts. On the surface, nothing seems too out of place, right? Then, your boss throws a curveball at you—there's no hard deadline for this project. At first, you might think of the lax timeline as something that would work in your favor. After all, no hard deadline means no rushing to finish. As time drags on, however, you find that you've hit a lull in your work. All of the moving details become tedious and exhausting, turning into barriers to your success rather than opportunities to display your skills. Even though this is an important project, you've already run out of steam—seemingly for no reason.

So, how do we eat the whale, so to speak? The key is starting small. A couple of bites a day soon add up to more than we could ever imagine. This approach makes dealing with obstacles far easier. Instead of piling onto already-full plates, barriers become easier to deal with when we're consistent with our efforts. With this in mind, it's crucial to remember that you don't have to do everything all in one day. Assertiveness doesn't magically appear in our lives, and slowly working towards our goals will make it far easier to overcome obstacles.

We deal with dozens of minor barriers every day. From last-minute tasks added to our workloads to literal construction barriers on our way to work, obstacles are unavoidable. Most of the time, we're able to navigate our way around these problems, giving them only a few seconds of our time and attention. However, there are some problems that we just can't seem to face head-on. For many of us, the overwhelm that accompanies the problems that we don't want to face is simply too much. As a result, we avoid facing these problems at all.

In psychology, this behavior is called avoidance. *Avoidance* is an unhelpful coping mechanism that allows the mind to escape from uncomfortable thoughts, feelings, and experiences. While it might seem beneficial to avoid discomfort, this approach prevents addressing the root of the problem. Instead, avoidance can lead to a cycle of behavior that worsens anxiety and depression, making it more difficult to solve problems, cope, and heal.

For instance, a person feeling depressed might struggle to get out of bed in the morning and start avoiding daily responsibilities that feel overwhelming. They might stay in bed until noon, skip breakfast, neglect to pay bills, and miss their gym session. When they eventually get up, they have less energy and time to handle their responsibilities. This lack of energy and time often leads to more negative thoughts and feelings, prompting further avoidant behavior and perpetuating the cycle of depression.

Chronic avoidance can sometimes turn into something even more pernicious— procrastination. Procrastination can take a heavy toll on your emotional, professional, personal, and social life, leaving you feeling exhausted and more overwhelmed than you were to begin with. Knowing that about 20% of people are classified as chronic procrastinators, according to the American Psychological Association, it's clear that many people have fallen into the trap of avoidance when it comes to dealing with unmanageable obstacles (Meyer, n.d.).

The need for assertiveness in your life, though undoubtedly beneficial, doesn't create immediate pressure. This makes it easy to avoid issues related to assertiveness, leading to procrastination and potential stagnation in your growth journey.

Stopping procrastination requires understanding its root causes and implementing practical strategies to overcome it. One effective approach is to break tasks into smaller, more manageable steps. When a task feels overwhelming, it's easy to put it off. However, by dividing it into smaller parts, each step becomes more approachable and less intimidating. Creating a detailed plan with specific deadlines for each step can provide a clear roadmap and reduce the feeling of being overwhelmed. Using tools like to-do lists, calendars, and reminders can help keep track of progress and maintain focus on the tasks at hand.

Another key strategy is to cultivate a conducive work environment and establish productive habits. Minimizing distractions is crucial. This might involve turning off notifications, creating a dedicated workspace, or using apps that block distracting websites.

Developing a routine can also help build momentum. For instance, setting aside specific times each day for focused work can train the brain to be more productive during those periods. Incorporating regular breaks is equally important, as it prevents burnout and maintains overall productivity.

Moreover, practicing self-compassion and rewarding oneself for completing tasks can boost motivation. This reinforces positive behavior, making it easier to stay on track and overcome procrastination.

As hard as it might seem to adopt assertiveness into your habits and behaviors, assertive communication remains in your grasp. As long as you persist in your efforts, you'll notice growth in the quality of your communication efforts.

Assertive communication is valuable, but several common barriers can hinder it in different contexts. One significant barrier is fear of conflict or confrontation. Many people avoid assertive communication because they worry about how others will react or fear causing tension or disagreement. This fear often leads individuals to default to passive communication styles, where they may avoid expressing their true thoughts and feelings to maintain harmony or avoid discomfort.

Another barrier is low self-esteem or lack of self-confidence. When individuals do not feel confident in their abilities or worth, they may struggle to assert their needs and opinions assertively. This can manifest as passive communication, where they may downplay their own needs or defer to others' preferences without speaking up for themselves.

Cultural or societal norms can also act as barriers to assertive communication. Different cultures and social backgrounds may have varying expectations about communication styles, politeness norms, and the acceptability of expressing assertiveness. This can lead individuals to adopt communication patterns that are more passive or aggressive depending on their cultural context.

Moreover, past negative experiences or conditioning can also be barriers. If individuals have experienced rejection, hurtful criticism, or negative consequences in the past when asserting themselves, they may develop a fear of asserting their needs in the future. This can create hesitancy or reluctance to engage in assertive communication, even when it may be beneficial or necessary.

In today's day and age, terms like "multiculturalism" and "diversity" are generally viewed as nothing more than buzzwords that organizations and individuals use to paint themselves in a positive light. However, this is not entirely true. There is still significant meaning behind the idea of multiculturalism, one that is growing increasingly important as our society grows and changes.

The term "multiculturalism" may have different connotations depending on where you look. Sociologists, cultural researchers, and politicians all have views on what multiculturalism is. This will undoubtedly change the definition over time, but for now, we can think of multiculturalism as referring to society's attitudes toward people of different ethnic, racial, or religious backgrounds.

Multiculturalism is vital in today's interconnected world. It enriches societies and promotes understanding among diverse groups. Embracing multiculturalism acknowledges and celebrates the unique identities, traditions, languages, and perspectives that individuals from different cultural backgrounds bring to a community or society. This diversity fosters a rich tapestry of experiences and knowledge, contributing to innovation, creativity, and social cohesion.

One key importance of multiculturalism lies in its role in promoting tolerance and acceptance. By exposing individuals to different cultures, multiculturalism challenges stereotypes, prejudices, and ethnocentric biases. It encourages people to recognize the humanity and dignity of others, regardless of their cultural heritage or background. This fosters empathy, respect, and a sense of global citizenship, essential for building peaceful and inclusive societies.

Moreover, multiculturalism enhances cultural exchange and learning. It allows individuals to learn from each other's traditions, customs, and practices, broadening their perspectives and enriching their personal growth. Exposure to diverse viewpoints encourages critical thinking and creativity, as people are exposed to new ideas and ways of approaching challenges.

Economically, multiculturalism contributes to a dynamic workforce and marketplace. It brings together individuals with diverse skills, experiences, and networks, which can lead to innovation and competitiveness in industries and businesses. Multicultural teams often demonstrate greater adaptability and problem-solving abilities, as they draw from a wider range of perspectives and solutions.

Ultimately, embracing multiculturalism promotes social justice and equity by advocating for the rights and representation of marginalized or minority groups. It encourages policies and practices that ensure equal opportunities and access to resources for all individuals, regardless of their cultural background.

Multiculturalism is not just a recognition of diversity; it is a commitment to inclusivity, mutual respect, and the celebration of human differences. Embracing multiculturalism enriches societies, promotes global understanding, and paves the way for a more harmonious and prosperous future for all.

Being assertive in a multicultural situation requires sensitivity, adaptability, and a deep understanding of cultural differences. Here are several strategies to effectively navigate assertiveness in such contexts:

Recognizing these barriers is the first step in overcoming them. Building self-confidence, learning assertive communication skills, understanding cultural differences, and addressing past conditioning through practice and support can help individuals navigate these barriers and communicate assertively in various aspects of their lives.

To overcome the more general barriers to assertive communication, individuals can take several proactive steps. First, addressing a fear of conflict or confrontation involves reframing perceptions. It's important to recognize that assertive communication is about expressing oneself respectfully, not about creating conflict. Practice assertiveness in low-stakes situations first, gradually building confidence in handling more challenging conversations. Developing conflict resolution skills can also help manage any discomfort that may arise.

Improving self-esteem and self-confidence is another key strategy. Engage in self-affirmation exercises to boost self-belief and recognize personal worth. Setting achievable goals for assertive communication and celebrating successes along the way can further reinforce confidence.

Understanding cultural or societal norms that influence communication styles is crucial, especially in diverse environments. Learn to adapt assertive communication techniques while respecting cultural differences. Seek guidance or training to navigate cultural nuances effectively.

Addressing past negative experiences involves recognizing that past reactions do not dictate future outcomes. Challenge negative beliefs about assertiveness and replace them with positive affirmations. Seek support from trusted individuals or professionals if necessary to work through lingering anxieties or barriers. Through persistence and practice, individuals can gradually overcome these barriers and communicate assertively with greater ease and effectiveness in various aspects of their lives.

Perhaps one of the most effective steps you can take to harden yourself against obstacles is to build up your mental and emotional resilience. *Resilience* refers to the ability to adapt and bounce back from adversity, trauma, or significant stress. It involves coping effectively with challenges, maintaining a positive outlook, and continuing to function and grow despite difficult circumstances. Resilience is characterized by emotional strength, flexibility, and the capacity to navigate setbacks and hardships with resilience.

Building resilience involves developing skills and adopting strategies that strengthen your ability to cope with adversity and bounce back from setbacks.

By integrating these strategies into your life, you can strengthen your resilience and develop the ability to navigate life's challenges with greater confidence, adaptability, and emotional strength. Building resilience is a lifelong process that empowers you to thrive and flourish, even in the face of adversity.

As you might've noticed, I use terms like "day-to-day" and "daily" quite a bit. While it might seem like a small detail, it hones in on a crucial aspect of assertiveness—consistency. In the next chapter, we'll explore the importance of daily assertiveness practices, as well as some techniques to get you started.

Chapter 8:

Practicing Daily Assertiveness

Changing your behavior when it comes to communication styles can be remarkably challenging. This is due to several interrelated factors. Firstly, behaviors often become habits over time, reinforced by routine and familiarity. These habits create neural pathways in the brain, making them automatic and difficult to change. The comfort and predictability of established behaviors provide a sense of security, and disrupting these patterns can feel uncomfortable and unsettling. Overcoming this inertia requires not only conscious effort but also a sustained commitment to new, often unfamiliar actions.

Another significant obstacle to changing behavior is emotional and psychological resistance to change. According to business consultant and author Rick Maurer, our response to change—while not always beneficial to us—is completely natural. "Resistance is in the eye of the beholder. The people resisting don't see what they are doing as resistance," he says. "They often see it as survival" (Maurer, 2021, p. 7).

People may fear the unknown or potential failure, leading to anxiety and self-doubt. This fear can be compounded by past experiences of unsuccessful attempts at change, reinforcing a belief that change is unattainable. People might also struggle with low self-efficacy, doubting their ability to effect change and persist through challenges.

Concerning communication styles, all of this can make it seem like there's no wiggle room for change. From this perspective, aggression and passivity just won't budge, and assertiveness can seem unattainable.

It's true to some extent—like any habit, behavior, or mindset, adopting assertiveness is a significant change. As we've discussed, there's no quick fix for becoming assertive. It requires a comprehensive life change built on a solid foundation of knowledge. You might initially have a strong desire to become truly assertive but later encounter a roadblock or plateau.

To get yourself out of this rut, you need to regularly reconnect with your "why;" the underlying reasons and passions driving your goal of becoming more assertive. To stoke the flames and keep your "why" alive for the long haul, you need consistency. Building routines, experimenting with different techniques, and reflecting on your situation are key, particularly regarding the frequency at which you do these things. To help you get started, we'll look at how to build a daily action plan that works for you, as well as some methods that can keep you inspired and motivated.

Creating an Assertiveness Action Plan

Creating a daily assertiveness practice involves integrating specific exercises and habits into your routine to develop and reinforce assertive communication skills over time. Start by setting clear intentions for your practice, such as becoming more comfortable expressing your needs and boundaries. Begin each day with positive affirmations that reinforce your self-worth and readiness to communicate assertively.

A practical step in daily assertiveness practice is to identify one or two situations each day where you can practice assertive communication. This could be speaking up in a meeting to share your ideas or concerns, respectfully declining a request that exceeds your capacity, or giving constructive feedback to a colleague or friend. Approach these situations with a clear understanding of your objectives and desired outcomes, aiming to express yourself confidently and respectfully.

Reflect on your assertiveness practice at the end of each day. Take note of what went well and where you may have felt challenged. Celebrate your successes and identify areas for improvement. Use these reflections to adjust your approach and set new goals for the next day or week.

Consistency and perseverance are key to developing assertiveness as a habit. Commit to practicing regularly. Gradually expand the scope of your assertiveness practice to include more challenging situations as you grow more comfortable and confident.

To get you thinking about what kinds of things you might do for your daily assertiveness practice, let's take a look at an exercise I like to call Devil's Advocate.

1. **Prepare.** Find a quiet space and set a timer for 5 minutes.

2. **Pick a hypothetical or real scenario.** Begin by recalling a recent situation where you wished you had been more assertive—perhaps a work-related scenario or a personal interaction. Visualize yourself in that situation again, taking on both your role and that of the other person involved.

3. **Play Devil's Advocate.** As yourself, practice expressing your thoughts, feelings, and needs assertively using "I" statements. Avoid being aggressive or passive.

Imagine the other person's responses and engage in a dialogue, focusing on clear communication and mutual understanding.

4. **Reflect.** Reflect on how it feels to assert yourself in this exercise. Note any challenges you encountered and how you managed them. Consider how you can apply what you've learned to real-life situations, aiming to assert your needs confidently while respecting others.

This exercise aims to strengthen your assertive communication skills in a supportive setting. By regularly practicing these techniques, you can build confidence and improve your ability to navigate challenging conversations effectively. If you're on the hunt for more in-depth exercises, look through the Exercises and Worksheets section and pick a few choices for your next daily assertiveness practice.

Real-Life Scenarios and the Benefits of Role-Playing

If you're interested in video games, you've probably played through a couple of role-playing games (RPGs) at some point. These video games are some of the most popular forms of entertainment on the market today, with titles like Fallout, Elden Ring, Skyrim, and The Witcher being some of the most notable from recent years.

Despite what some critics and culture commentators say, research has shown that RPGs can have massive benefits to player's cognitive and psychological health. For instance, one 2022 study looked at 2,200 young adult participants to see what observable effects RPG playtime had on cognitive functions.

The results were shocking. Researchers found that young adults who played RPG-style video games for around 20 hours per week had notably increased brain activity, specifically in areas of the brain associated with memory and impulse control (Charaani et. al., 2022). Other similar studies have pointed to RPG-style games' ability to increase hand-eye coordination, better judgment, and even gray matter (Cleveland Clinic, 2022).

This isn't isolated to virtual games. During the pandemic, physical role-playing games like Dungeons & Dragons saw a whopping 31% increase in sales, with the biggest consumers of RPGs being college-aged adults (van Doren, 2023). Whether virtual or in-person, RPGs allow players to collaborate, figure out complex tasks, and work towards manageable goals, cultivating a sense of accomplishment and community.

Of course, I don't say any of this to convince you to start playing video games. What video games and traditional RPGs tell us, however, is that role-playing can do wonders for our cognitive, emotional, and psychological health. Whether you're alone or with people you trust, role-playing in the context of gaining assertiveness can boost your self-image, grow your confidence, and make you feel better about future stressful conversations. Role-playing isn't about talking to yourself in the bathroom mirror—it's about giving yourself a sense of agency in the face of something overwhelming.

Role-playing before a stressful situation offers significant psychological benefits by helping individuals prepare mentally and emotionally for challenging interactions or scenarios. Engaging in role-playing allows you to simulate the situation in a controlled environment, providing an opportunity to anticipate potential challenges and practice assertive communication techniques. This process helps reduce anxiety and build confidence by familiarizing yourself with different responses and outcomes.

Psychologically, role-playing activates cognitive processes that enhance problem-solving skills and decision-making abilities. By immersing yourself in a hypothetical scenario, you can experiment with various approaches and strategies to determine the most effective course of action. This practice strengthens mental flexibility and adaptability, which are crucial for managing unexpected or high-pressure situations with composure.

Moreover, role-playing promotes self-awareness and self-reflection. It allows you to identify strengths and areas for improvement in your communication style, assertiveness, and emotional regulation. Through constructive feedback and reflection on the role-playing experience, you can refine your skills and develop a more nuanced understanding of how to navigate complex interpersonal interactions effectively. Ultimately, role-playing serves as a valuable psychological tool for enhancing readiness, resilience, and performance in real-life stressful situations.

Incorporating role-playing into your daily assertiveness practice can significantly enhance your ability to handle challenging situations with confidence and clarity. Each day, identify specific scenarios or conversations where you anticipate needing to assert yourself or communicate effectively. Take a few moments to mentally prepare by visualizing the interaction and considering different responses or approaches you could take.

Engage in role-playing by physically or mentally rehearsing the conversation. Act out both your assertive responses and potential reactions from the other party. This exercise allows you to anticipate various outcomes and practice adjusting your communication style accordingly.

By simulating the scenario beforehand, you can identify any potential pitfalls or challenges and develop strategies to address them assertively. Psychologically, role-playing helps desensitize anxiety about assertive communication by creating a safe space to practice and refine your skills. It builds confidence as you become more familiar with assertive behaviors and effective communication techniques.

After each role-playing session, reflect on what went well and areas for improvement. Use this feedback to adjust your approach and further refine your assertiveness practice.

Over time, integrating role-playing into your daily assertiveness practice strengthens your ability to navigate difficult conversations with composure and clarity. It enhances your problem-solving abilities, emotional resilience, and overall effectiveness in assertive communication. This ultimately leads to more positive outcomes in both personal and professional interactions.

Now that we've explored some techniques for daily assertiveness, it's time to consider some of the wider psychological factors that assertiveness can impact. In the next chapter, we'll take a look at our emotions—what they do for us, how we can navigate them, and how our emotions interact with assertiveness.

Chapter 9:

Assertiveness and Emotional

Intelligence

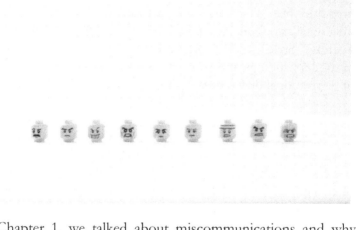

In Chapter 1, we talked about miscommunications and why they happen. What we did not discuss, however, are the emotions and reactions that can accompany instances of this. Let's examine a bizarre and increasingly popular manifestation of this in popular culture: texting lingo.

Written miscommunications happen all the time, but SMS miscommunications are probably some of the most common. This is especially true when one party is older and another party is younger. Different generations have a demonstrably wide variety of communication methods when texting, which are often perceived negatively by those of differing ages. As research has shown, older people tend to use traditional punctuation and fewer emojis, while younger people tend to forego punctuation while simultaneously sending longer messages (Broadwater, 2023). The problem here comes down to intent versus perception, a key part of miscommunication that we talked about in Chapter 1. Periods at the end of every sentence in a message, for example, are usually interpreted as a sign of anger by younger generations. Older folks, however, don't think twice about using proper punctuation.

Even if you haven't experienced this type of digital misunderstanding for yourself, you might find that the articles written on the topic still resonate with your age group. Blog post titles like "The Way You Text Reveals if You're a Boomer, Millennial, or Gen Z" and "You Are Only as Old as Your Texting Style" detail accounts of the wide array of misunderstandings and trod-on-toes that often arise as a result of generational differences.

In the real world, these kinds of stereotypes about age aren't universal. Of course, not all Baby Boomers hate emojis, and a good portion of Millennials still use proper grammar when texting. It's important to avoid over-generalizing entire swaths of the population, as this can occasionally lead to even more miscommunications.

However, in the virtual world, we see the stereotypical differences between generations all over the place, perhaps more so because the people who address these differences are passionate about their way of communicating. So, when a Millennial sees a message from a Baby Boomer with no emojis and a period after each sentence, this violates some of the social norms that younger generations have around texting. From a Millennial perspective, it feels like a given that the Baby Boomer is angry about something or maybe doesn't want to continue the conversation. From the perspective of a Baby

Boomer, however, all of the emojis and exclamation marks can make Millennials seem very, very excited for no discernable reason.

One reason for this is awareness. We aren't always aware of the social norms of people from a different background than us. The other, possibly more relevant culprit, however, is the emotional intelligence associated with our awareness of how other people feel.

Emotional intelligence (EI) plays a crucial role in personal and professional success by encompassing the ability to recognize, understand, and manage emotions—both in oneself and others. One key aspect of EI is self-awareness, which involves recognizing your own emotions and understanding how they affect your thoughts and behaviors. This awareness allows individuals to make informed decisions, manage stress effectively, and maintain a positive outlook even in challenging situations.

Another vital component of EI is empathy. *Empathy* is the ability to understand and consider others' emotions, perspectives, and feelings. Empathy fosters meaningful connections and enhances interpersonal relationships by promoting understanding, trust, and cooperation. It enables individuals to communicate effectively, resolve conflicts diplomatically, and support others in times of need.

Furthermore, EI includes the skill of emotional regulation. This involves managing and expressing emotions appropriately. This skill is essential in maintaining composure, adapting to change, and making rational decisions under pressure.

Individuals with high EI are often more resilient and adaptable. They can navigate complex social dynamics and respond thoughtfully to diverse situations. Overall, cultivating EI is crucial for fostering personal well-being, building strong relationships, and achieving success.

Understanding Emotional Intelligence

Understanding the concept of emotional intelligence (EI) begins with recognizing its multifaceted nature and the impact it has on personal and professional interactions. At its core, EI involves the ability to perceive, understand, manage, and utilize emotions effectively. The good news is that you've already started back in Chapter 3 by developing self-awareness and recognizing your own emotions, strengths, and weaknesses, and how these influence your behavior and decisions. This introspective process helps you identify patterns in your emotional responses and understand their underlying causes.

Next, focus on enhancing your ability to recognize and understand emotions in others. This aspect of EI, often referred to as empathy, involves actively listening to others, observing non-verbal cues, and considering their perspectives and feelings. Cultivating empathy allows you to build rapport, strengthen relationships, and respond empathetically to others' emotions, fostering trust and mutual understanding.

Additionally, practice emotional regulation, which involves constructively managing your emotions. This includes controlling impulsive reactions, staying calm under pressure, and expressing emotions appropriately.

It's worth mentioning that staying calm is often easier said than done. If you've recently been in any kind of emotionally fraught situation, you might be aware of how the phrase "calm down" can be extremely inflammatory for some people. In the same way, simply telling yourself to "stay calm" can actually make you feel even less calm!

This is especially important for those who suffer from anxiety of any kind. According to Karen Ephlin, a pediatrician at Geisinger Healthcare, "Saying 'calm down' assumes that [anxieties] can be wished way and isn't a real issue in the first place. If someone is having an anxiety attack, you're better off reassuring them and talking to them about positive things" (Geisinger, 2017, p. 6).

Instead of writing off our feelings, we must take steps to regulate ourselves. This means doing things like deep breathing, journaling, and even daily activities like working out, eating healthily, and taking care of our mental health.

Motivation and Emotional Intelligence

Motivation is a complicated and storied field in the realm of psychology and neuroscience. The study of motivation has evolved significantly over time, reflecting changing perspectives and approaches in psychology and related disciplines. The earliest discussions on motivation can be traced back to ancient Greek philosophers such as Plato and Aristotle, who explored the concepts of human desires, needs, and drives. However, systematic study began in the late 19th and early 20th centuries with the emergence of psychology as a scientific discipline.

In the late 19th century, psychologists such as William James and William McDougall proposed instinct theories of motivation. They suggested that behaviors are driven by innate instincts or biological urges that compel individuals to act in certain ways to satisfy basic needs or drives.

This later morphed into *drive reduction theory*. Developed in the 1930s by Clark Hull and others, drive reduction theory posited that motivation arises from the need to reduce physiological drives such as hunger, thirst, or arousal. According to this theory, organisms are motivated to engage in behaviors that reduce these internal tensions and restore homeostasis.

In the mid-20th century, humanistic psychologists like Abraham Maslow and Carl Rogers introduced theories emphasizing higher-order needs and self-actualization. Maslow's hierarchy of needs proposed that human motivation is hierarchical, with basic physiological needs at the bottom and self-actualization at the top. This perspective shifted focus from biological drives to the pursuit of personal growth and fulfillment.

In the 1960s and 1970s, cognitive psychologists such as Albert Bandura and Edward Deci expanded the study of motivation to include cognitive processes and social factors. Bandura's *social learning theory* emphasized the role of observational learning and self-efficacy in motivating behavior, while Deci's *self-determination theory* highlighted the importance of intrinsic motivation and autonomy in driving behavior.

Today, the study of motivation encompasses a broad range of theories and perspectives, including cognitive, social, evolutionary, and neuroscientific approaches. Researchers explore how motivation is influenced by factors such as beliefs, emotions, incentives, social context, and neural processes. Motivation research is interdisciplinary, drawing on insights from psychology, neuroscience, economics, sociology, and organizational behavior.

Why is this important? Motivation, assertive behaviors, and emotional intelligence are intertwined. They all significantly influence how individuals navigate personal and professional interactions.

Motivation serves as the driving force behind assertive behaviors, influencing individuals to express their needs, opinions, and boundaries effectively. Whether stemming from intrinsic desires like personal values and goals or extrinsic factors such as rewards and recognition, motivation plays a pivotal role in shaping assertiveness. Motivated individuals are more likely to confidently advocate for themselves or others, even in challenging circumstances, thereby fostering clear communication and proactive engagement in interpersonal dynamics.

Emotional intelligence complements assertive behaviors by providing the emotional awareness and regulation necessary for effective communication. It involves recognizing and managing one's own emotions, understanding others' feelings, and navigating relationships with empathy and social acumen. Individuals with high EI are adept at balancing assertiveness with sensitivity to others' perspectives, ensuring that their assertive actions are communicated respectfully and with consideration for emotional dynamics.

Assertive behaviors, in turn, are closely linked to EI as they require a nuanced understanding of one's own emotions and those of others. Assertiveness hinges on self-awareness to identify personal needs and feelings, self-management to regulate emotional responses, social awareness to perceive others' emotions accurately, and relationship management to communicate assertively while maintaining positive interactions. This integration of EI enhances individuals' ability to navigate conflicts, foster collaborative relationships, and achieve mutual goals through assertive communication.

When effectively integrated, motivation, assertive behaviors, and EI form a cohesive framework for personal and professional success. Motivation propels individuals to engage assertively, while EI equips them with the skills to manage emotions, empathize with others, and navigate complex social dynamics. Together, these elements foster resilience, adaptability, and effective leadership, contributing to positive outcomes in diverse contexts from interpersonal relationships to organizational settings.

Developing Emotional Intelligence

Developing emotional intelligence (EI) involves deliberate practice and self-awareness to enhance your ability to understand and manage emotions effectively. Start by increasing your self-awareness through reflection and introspection. Pay attention to your emotions, triggers, and patterns of behavior in different situations. Journaling can be a helpful tool to track your emotions and identify recurring themes or challenges.

Next, work on improving your empathy by actively listening to others and trying to understand their perspectives and emotions. Practice putting yourself in their shoes and considering how they might feel. Engage in meaningful conversations that allow you to connect on an emotional level and practice responding empathetically to others' experiences.

Emotional regulation is another critical aspect of developing EI. Learn to manage stress and control your emotional reactions by practicing relaxation techniques such as deep breathing, mindfulness, or meditation. Recognize when you are experiencing strong emotions and take steps to calm yourself before responding. Developing resilience to setbacks and challenges also strengthens emotional regulation, as it helps you bounce back and maintain focus on your goals despite obstacles.

Continuously seek feedback from others to gain insights into how your emotions and behavior impact them. Use constructive feedback to refine your communication style and interpersonal skills. By committing to ongoing self-improvement and practicing these strategies consistently, you can cultivate a higher level of EI that enhances your relationships, decision-making abilities, and overall well-being.

Alone, that can be a lot to tackle. The key to developing big skills like EI is to break them up into smaller, more manageable pieces, which we can easily do with basic writing and other activities.

1. on **Mindfulness Meditation:** Engage in regular mindfulness meditation to increase self-awareness and emotional regulation. Focus on observing your thoughts, emotions, and bodily sensations without judgment. This practice strengthens your ability to recognize and manage emotions effectively.

2. **Journaling:** Keep a journal to reflect on your emotions, experiences, and interpersonal interactions. Write about challenging situations, noting your emotional responses and the outcomes. Analyze patterns in your emotional reactions to gain insights into your triggers and behaviors.

3. **Emotion Recognition Practice:** Practice identifying emotions in yourself and others. Use facial expressions, body language, and vocal tones to discern different emotional states. Engage in role-playing scenarios to improve your ability to recognize and respond empathetically to others' emotions.

4. **Active Listening Exercises:** Enhance your empathy and social skills by practicing active listening. Focus on fully understanding the speaker's message without

interrupting or formulating responses prematurely. Reflect what you hear to confirm understanding and validate the speaker's emotions.

5. **Gratitude Practice:** Cultivate positive emotions and resilience by practicing gratitude. Regularly write down three things you are grateful for each day. This exercise helps shift your focus from negative emotions to positive experiences, fostering emotional balance and well-being.

6. **Self-Compassion Exercises:** Develop self-compassion by treating yourself with kindness and understanding during challenging times. Practice self-soothing techniques, such as positive self-talk or self-care activities, to nurture your emotional resilience and self-esteem.

7. **Feedback Seeking:** Seek feedback from trusted individuals to gain insights into your strengths and areas for growth. Be open to constructive criticism and use it as an opportunity for self-improvement. Actively listen to feedback without becoming defensive, and consider how you can apply it to enhance your emotional intelligence skills.

8. **Empathy Building Activities:** Engage in activities that promote empathy, such as volunteering or participating in community events. Connect with diverse individuals and learn about their experiences to broaden your perspective and deepen your understanding of others' emotions.

9. **Personal Values Exploration:** Reflect on your core values and how they influence your emotions and behaviors. Align your actions with your values to foster authenticity and integrity in your interactions with

others. This exercise strengthens self-awareness and enhances emotional resilience.

By incorporating these exercises into your daily routine, you can cultivate EI skills that support personal growth, enhance relationships, and contribute to your overall well-being. Regular practice and reflection are key to developing and strengthening your emotional intelligence over time.

Applying Emotional Intelligence in Assertive Communication

The second layer of mastering assertiveness is understanding that others are going through the same struggle as you. At the same time, it's important to recognize that you might be in a different place than others when it comes to communicating assertively. While the people you interact with may not be communicating effectively, you must maintain the integrity of your assertiveness.

This boils down to a concept in psychology called the *locus of control*, or the extent to which you believe your actions can influence the outcomes you see. In 1954, psychologist Julian Rotter developed this concept as somewhat of a binary. In any given situation, you either possess an external locus of control (in which you have no control over the outcome of a situation), or you possess an internal locus of control (in which your actions can control the outcomes you see). Having an internal or external locus of control isn't a good-versus-bad scenario, and each mindset has merits in different situations. However, some studies have shown that those with a consistent internal locus of control often lead people to feel more confident, more independent, and happier overall (Cherry, 2024a).

In the context of assertive communication, it's ultimately up to you to decide whether your communication style is within your control or not. To give you a hint, it's not the latter. What is definitely outside your control, however, are the emotions and behaviors of others. Even when the people you interact with aren't managing their emotions, it's your responsibility to keep calm and continue being assertive.

Emotional intelligence (EI) and assertive communication are closely intertwined, each complementing and reinforcing the other in interpersonal interactions. Assertive communication relies on EI to effectively express one's thoughts, feelings, and needs while respecting the emotions and rights of others. Individuals with high EI can accurately perceive their own emotions and those of others, which is essential for understanding when and how to assert themselves appropriately.

A key component of assertive communication is self-awareness, a foundational skill of EI. Self-awareness allows individuals to recognize their emotions, triggers, and communication styles, enabling them to assert themselves confidently and authentically. Understanding one's emotions helps in managing them effectively during assertive interactions, preventing emotional reactions that could undermine communication.

Moreover, empathy, another critical aspect of EI, supports assertive communication by facilitating understanding and consideration of others' perspectives and emotions. Empathetic individuals are better able to communicate assertively without being perceived as aggressive or dismissive, as they can navigate conversations with sensitivity and respect. They listen actively, validate others' feelings, and express their thoughts and boundaries clearly, fostering mutual understanding and constructive dialogue.

Overall, the relationship between EI and assertive communication highlights how developing EI skills enhances the effectiveness and impact of assertive communication in various personal and professional contexts.

You might remember the bizarre question from back in Chapter 3 How do you eat a whale? Our answer—one bite at a time—is important to remember going forward. By now, we have a pretty solid foundation, built by scaffolding techniques like self-awareness, self-esteem, and now, emotional intelligence. This foundation can now support some of the more advanced aspects of assertiveness, allowing us to realize our full potential when it comes to communication.

In the next chapter, we'll explore some of these advanced techniques, as well as the situations in which they might be useful.

Chapter 10:

Advanced Assertiveness

Techniques

Now that you have a strong base of knowledge about the myriad aspects of assertive communication, it's time to delve into some of the deeper psychological tools that we can use on ourselves and others when we need a little extra pizzazz. For this purpose, we'll take a closer look at two different areas that nicely accompany assertive communication: positive language and conflict resolution.

The Power of Positive Language

Positive language refers to communication that is constructive, supportive, and uplifting. It involves using words and phrases that convey optimism, encouragement, and affirmation. Doing this creates a favorable and empowering environment for both the speaker and the listener.

Chances are, you've probably heard of the pink elephant conundrum. On the off chance that you haven't, however, let's run through the exercise. To start, try to clear your mind of everything—worries, plans, and ruminations about the future or past. The only rule in this scenario is to follow instructions. The first instruction is simple: *don't* think of a giant pink elephant. Don't picture the pink elephant standing right next to you, and definitely don't imagine that it's also wearing hot pink polish on its toenails. Sit with these instructions for about 30 seconds or so. Did you think of the pink elephant?

You probably did. Don't worry—thinking of the pink elephant is hardwired into our collective psyche, and following the instructions is impossible in a certain sense. This highlights an important aspect of how the words we choose interact with our thought processes. Even if we cognitively know that the instructions expressly said to *not* think of the elephant, our brains still do the one thing we expressly forbade them to do.

Why does this happen, exactly? Well, it's easy to visualize the world around us. Since the beginning of our species, we've relied on clues from the observable world to tell us what's safe and what's unsafe. We have a built-in function that allows us to see things in our mind's eye. Several intricate parts make up this complex biological system, but here are the main brain areas that let us imagine things in our heads:

- The frontal cortex controls our perception of instructions.

- The temporal lobe influences how we identify physical things.

- The parietal cortex controls autobiographical memory.

- The primary visual cortex is used when we imagine detailed, tangible items in our heads.

In the case of the pink elephant, all of these brain systems were in play. As you might notice, there's no biological function that controls *not* doing something. In short, we're not built to deal with the absence of something.

In the context of assertiveness, this idea has massive implications for the words that you use with yourself and others on a day-to-day basis. For instance, saying "don't worry" to yourself before presenting in a big meeting won't be effective in lowering your stress levels. This is where positive language comes into play. Rather than saying "Don't worry," say something more specific and intentional, like "You are well-prepared for this meeting, and you'll do great!"

Positive Language and Persuasion in the Context of Assertiveness

When we consider positive language in the real world, there are several things to take into account. For one, it's important to remember that positive language isn't a secret superpower. It won't always get you what you want, and positive language alone won't always be enough to change how others respond to you. With that being said, positive language can have a staggering effect on your daily interactions, especially when navigating tricky situations.

- **Use persuasive techniques ethically.** No matter what your aims are when you try to persuade someone, it's important to consider the ethics and morality of what you're saying. This is where assertiveness, particularly empathy, fairness, and honesty, come into play. Using positive language doesn't give you a license to compromise on being honest with someone else. You should always try to be upfront about your intentions. For instance, say you're trying to persuade a friend to split the bill with you after dinner when you normally pay for everything. Instead of being passive-aggressive and heading to the bathroom when they see the bill coming, a truly effective (and more persuasive) communicator would initiate a conversation about money by being truthful about what they need. This kind of honesty doesn't need to be a sit-down, formal occasion. A quick phrase like "I'd really like us to start splitting bills when we go out to dinner" is enough to get the ball rolling. It's also important to consider what's fair to the other person. Before trying to persuade someone, take a step back and look at your motivations, expectations, and desired outcomes to ensure that you're taking everyone into account.

- **Influence outcomes.** When we try to persuade someone, we're usually asking for something. Whether it's a piece of information, an action, or a favor, the way we phrase questions and reasoning can drastically impact how others respond to your wants and needs. Imagine that you're asking a colleague at work to change the tone of their emails. Instead of starting with a critique like, "I think the tone of your emails is unprofessional," a positive language approach would start with something more along the lines of, "I would like to see you use XYZ language in your emails. Is there a time when we could look at some examples together?" This principle extends beyond the workplace and into other aspects of your life. Imagine that you ask to move in with your romantic partner, but they want to stay in their place. Instead of saying, "Why don't you want to move in with me?" try saying something like, "I'd really like to take our relationship to the next step. Can we talk about this more?" It would likely be more effective.

- **Avoid negativity.** Of course, positive language entails that you stay away from the negatives. Instead of *nots* and *don'ts,* finding ways to paint things in a positive light is crucial. However, there's another layer to this principle. When you're trying to persuade someone, you want to stay away from anything that might bring up negative connotations, triggers, or defensive reactions. In short, we want to identify all the phrases like "Calm down" that could be perceived as offensive or negative. This will ultimately look different for every situation, which means that you'll need to sit down and identify any potential potholes in the conversation. There are some universal negatives to avoid, though. For example, any apology that is followed by a "but" is usually perceived as a slap-dash attempt to shift blame.

In addition to positive language, there are several other persuasive techniques that you can use while building your assertiveness. For our purposes, we'll look at seven different tools, created by psychologist Dr. Robert B. Cialdini (Schenker, 2022):

1. Reciprocity, or giving something with the expectation of getting something back from someone. You can think of this as a quid-pro-quo, like offering to drive a friend to the airport in exchange for them watching your dog for a day.

2. Commitment, or our desire to be seen as consistent by other people. This entails getting people to commit to very small things, like letting you borrow a pen or letting you buy coffee, which then grows into bigger commitments over time.

3. Social proof, or the idea that we like to blend in. If you're able to persuade one or two people to see your point of view, you're more likely to convince others. In short, you'll be more persuasive if you have people on your side.

4. Authority, or the tendency for people to respond to authoritative figures. If you're a doctor, for instance, you'll likely be able to convince people about the effects of a certain drug based on your professional background. If you have any authority on a matter, try using it to your benefit.

5. Liking, or the idea that people will agree with you more if they like you. Before you try to persuade someone, try to find common ground with them. Get to know them and build rapport with them.

6. Scarcity, or the sense of FOMO that we talked about a few chapters ago. When you're persuading someone, try creating a sense of scarcity by highlighting tight timelines, the benefits of your ideas, or anything else that would draw someone into listening to what you have to say.

7. Unity, or the idea that we can influence people if they align with us in a broader sense. If you're a member of a group, whether it's cultural, political, or social, bring it up before you try to persuade someone. This will build rapport and strengthen your relationship with that person. (Even if you don't get what you want.)

Conflict Resolution

To understand conflict resolution, we first have to understand the different roles that we can play in a conflict. While there are many frameworks to describe conflict dynamics, we'll take a look at five different roles:

1. **Competing (Assertive-Aggressive):** This style involves asserting one's own needs and goals at the expense of others. Individuals using this approach prioritize winning the conflict over maintaining relationships. To deal with this style, it's important to stay calm and assertive, clearly stating your own needs while seeking common ground. Focus on collaborative problem-solving to find mutually beneficial solutions.

2. **Avoiding (Passive):** People with this style sidestep conflicts and prefer to withdraw from disagreements. They often avoid addressing the underlying issues. To engage with avoiders, create a safe and supportive environment, gently encouraging them to share their thoughts and concerns. Emphasize the importance of resolving the issue for mutual benefit.

3. **Accommodating (Passive-Aggressive):** This style involves putting others' needs ahead of one's own while suppressing personal grievances. Accommodators may comply outwardly but harbor resentment. To address this, encourage open and honest communication. Validate their feelings and reassure them that their needs and opinions are valued.

4. **Collaborating (Assertive-Assertive):** Collaborative individuals seek win-win solutions by engaging in open dialogue and mutual problem-solving. They aim to satisfy both parties' needs. To work effectively with collaborators, foster an environment of trust and cooperation. Encourage brainstorming and creative thinking to find solutions that benefit everyone involved.

5. **Compromising (Assertive-Yielding):** Compromisers aim to find a middle ground by negotiating and making concessions. They seek quick resolutions that partially

satisfy both parties. When dealing with compromisers, focus on clear communication and fairness. Acknowledge their willingness to find a balanced solution and work together to reach an agreement that addresses the most important needs of both sides.

As you might be able to tell from the different conflict styles, conflict and conflict resolution have a lot to do with communication styles. This is an area where the assertive techniques we've learned about are tested most. With that in mind, trying to de-escalate a heated argument is perhaps not a good choice if you don't feel completely comfortable with your self-awareness, self-esteem, or other assertiveness factors. If you do feel comfortable, however, you may benefit from knowing more about conflict resolution in the context of what we've learned.

Now, resolving conflicts in the real world can seem a little daunting. Whether you're arguing with your spouse or discussing something with your boss, conflict can stir up negative emotions. However, with the right tools, conflicts don't have to turn into fights. To start, constructive conflicts possess many of the assertiveness tools that we've already talked about in previous chapters.

- Using "I" statements and avoiding criticism of yourself and others.

- Being honest about yourself, your intentions, and your needs.

- Displaying assertive body language like holding eye contact (when culturally appropriate), maintaining a good posture, and speaking with an even tone and volume.

- Avoiding meaningless statements and filler words like "um" and "okay."

In addition to these basics, there are conflict-specific assertiveness techniques that you should consider. Adding to your list of do's and don'ts, keep some of these tools in your back pocket.

- **Use strategic pauses.** Sometimes, the space between words is more important than the words themselves. If you're someone who tries to avoid awkward pauses in conversations, then strategic pausing is essential to master in the context of conflict resolution. These pauses don't have to be long or drawn out. A brief stop before or after an important word gets your point across much better than yelling ever could. For instance, consider the sentence, "We should take a moment to consider the benefits of option A." Now imagine yourself delivering this line in a meeting, placing a brief pause after the word "benefits." "We should take a moment to consider the *benefits*... of option A." This kind of pausing emphasizes the point you want to make without compromising your volume or tone of voice.

- **Be clear, confident, and controlled.** In a conflict, appearing confused, meek, and out of control can destroy your argument. (Even if it's a good one!) We've already discussed some basic techniques like smooth body language, self-esteem, and avoiding filler words. Now, it's time to turn these elements up to 11, so to speak. One of the best ways to accomplish this is to mirror the body language, speech, and vocabulary of calm parties in the conflict. This will show everyone that you're reasonable, willing to negotiate, but firm about your principles.

- **Don't be afraid to negotiate (and renegotiate).** In a negotiation or conflict, it's sometimes difficult to gauge how flexible the other party is. The reality is that we can never fully know what's happening in someone else's head, and we never fully know how much they're willing to compromise. When settling a conflict, don't assume the other party's limits. Saying "yes" to the first available solution is just as good as saying "no" to yourself! When you receive an offer or solution from the other party, consider it carefully before providing your response. Sometimes, it's even okay to take time away from the situation by saying something like, "Can we pause this talk? I'd like to think about what you just said some more." If you decide that a potential solution doesn't work for you, do your best to describe exactly what you take issue with by using "I" statements. Then, make a counter-offer and explicitly define your ask.

- **Don't let yourself be ignored.** If you come from a more passive communication style, it's sometimes easy to let yourself get talked over by others. Of course, this doesn't achieve your goals, and it won't result in a productive conflict. If you get ignored or interrupted, make sure to acknowledge it verbally without becoming defensive or emotional. To do this, phrases like, "Just a second, I'd like to finish my thought," "As I was saying, I believe..." and "As I mentioned earlier," are great ways to speak up for yourself while keeping the conflict respectful. It's also important to note that not all interruptions are intentionally disrespectful. In tense conflicts, people's passions sometimes get the better of them. Instead of getting frustrated or angry, consider the enthusiasm they have for the subject and try to get them back on track in a respectful way.

- **Command the floor.** In some conflicts, active listening gives way to shouting matches. When presenting your thoughts, don't give up people's attention until you've said what you want to say. When someone tries to interject while you're still speaking, use some of the phrases outlined above to keep attention on you. In this respect, body language is also important. Avoid doing things like crossing your arms. Use hand gestures and a tall, open posture instead.

- **Consider the image you project**. Sometimes, people in the workplace see us through a lens we're not even aware of. From interests, hobbies, social events, and even the way we speak, we're constantly building and rebuilding a picture of ourselves that others pick up on. For instance, someone who always makes self-deprecating jokes will probably be perceived as a weak negotiator in a conflict. In this way, all of the things you do in the workplace act as a kind of scaffolding that creates your treatment by others. Before a conflict begins, think carefully about the way you present yourself at work, and make sure that it aligns with the image you want to project.

None of these skills are easy to do. They may be the most difficult aspects of assertive communication that we've discussed so far. To ingrain these methods into your repertoire, you'll need to practice consistently and frequently through things like visualization techniques, journaling, role-playing, and even practicing in front of a mirror. As we know, language shapes our reality. By using language that aligns with these skills, you'll find that implementing them in real-world situations becomes far easier.

Mediating Conflicts Between Others

Depending on your job, personal life, and social circle, you may find yourself sandwiched between two conflicting parties.

Although you're not directly involved in a conflict, there are several ways you can use assertiveness to alleviate the pressure that conflicts can create.

1. **Staying Neutral:** Remain impartial and avoid taking sides. Ensure that each party feels heard and respected.

2. **Establishing Ground Rules:** Set clear guidelines for respectful communication, such as no interrupting, no personal attacks, and listening actively.

3. **Encouraging Open Communication:** Allow each party to express their perspectives and feelings without interruption. Encourage them to use "I" statements to avoid blame and to help them focus on their own experiences.

4. **Acknowledging Emotions:** Recognize and validate the emotions of both parties. This helps to build trust and shows that you understand their feelings.

5. **Clarifying Issues:** Identify the root causes of the conflict by asking open-ended questions. Summarize and reflect what you hear to ensure understanding.

6. **Promoting Active Listening:** Encourage each party to listen to the other's perspective without immediately planning their rebuttal.

7. **Summarizing and Agreeing on Action Steps:** Once a resolution is reached, summarize the agreed-upon steps and ensure both parties are clear on their responsibilities moving forward. Document the agreement if necessary.

By practicing these conflict resolution techniques consistently and adapting them to specific situations, individuals can effectively manage and resolve conflicts in a way that promotes understanding, cooperation, and constructive outcomes.

Skills like conflict resolution and positive language aren't easy to master. They take time, energy, and a conscious will to continue. However, these skills are essential, especially for those in high-communication or leadership positions. In the next chapter, we'll take a closer look at leadership roles, as well as some of the specific techniques that can improve your leadership in the workplace and beyond.

Chapter 11:

Assertiveness in Leadership

When Jane, a 40-year-old professional at a sales company, presented her new ideas to her team, she didn't expect them to be so rude.

At a regional retreat, she introduced her solution to an ongoing issue with their reporting system. This solution would, ideally, eventually be implemented across all regions of the company. She also expressed her desire to lead this new initiative. She demonstrated the key qualities of an assertive leader as previously described. She had the courage to initiate the process at the regional level, remained task-focused, and aimed to connect with her team to gain their support.

Her team consisted of three male colleagues, all of whom immediately rejected her idea on the basis that it would require too much energy and effort. Recalling the situation for an interview in *Forbes*, she said, "His voice was really loud. I felt pushed, and I felt a pulsating in my left ear, and my thoughts went blank" (Glabb, 2022, p. 13).

This alone would have been enough to make anyone feel terrible about themselves, but the situation became worse when two other colleagues joined the conversation. Unable to think and unable to stick up for herself, Jane soon found that her own team had ripped every part of her idea to shreds.

This is the kind of thing that dissuades people from trying to improve their communication styles. After all, if a rude colleague is going to tear down your ideas anyway, what's the point in making an effort to share them?

Of course, giving up is not an option. We know that, despite our occasional shortcomings, we have a lot to offer the world. While she was effectively silenced at the moment, Jane later went on to work on her ability to be assertive at work. She specifically focused on the areas that we've been talking about:

Soon after, Jane was able to present her ideas to an audience of engaged (and far less rude) listeners. She was then able to lead the charge when it came to improving her workplace and building and managing an effective team to achieve what she had originally planned.

Situations like the one Jane found herself in happen all the time. When they do, it's natural for us to fantasize about becoming the hero in our own story; about saying the perfect turn of phrase that will floor your audience and instantly get them to see your point of view.

This, of course, doesn't always happen. The lack of assertiveness in these situations can make you feel like a doormat. Cognitively, we know that this isn't true. We know that we all have valuable contributions to make to the world, and everyone has off days. Nevertheless, situations like Jane's still impact our confidence and performance in leadership roles.

Despite these terrible and disheartening setbacks, we often find ourselves standing at the threshold of leadership opportunities that will allow us to prove our salt. Studies have shown that assertiveness is a crucial skill for career advancement, and has been positively correlated with promotions (Laud & Johnson, 2012). In these moments, and in future leadership positions, holding strong to your beliefs and sticking to your guns is crucial.

Imagine that you're in Jane's position. What would you have done differently to prepare for potential pushback from coworkers? How would you have mitigated the negative responses?

When we talk about assertiveness in leadership, it's not enough to just throw in the occasional "I" statement or turn of phrase. To be an assertive leader, you have to adopt the characteristics that reinforce your leadership.

In addition to everything we've talked about so far, assertive leaders also have other main traits:

Incorporating assertive communication into your leadership style involves adopting a proactive approach to expressing your thoughts, decisions, and expectations clearly and confidently while respecting the perspectives and contributions of others. Start by cultivating self-awareness to understand your communication style and how it impacts others. Recognize situations where assertiveness is beneficial, such as when delegating tasks, providing feedback, or addressing conflicts. Practice active listening to understand the viewpoints and concerns of your team members fully. Acknowledge their input and demonstrate empathy to build trust and rapport. This approach encourages open dialogue and mutual respect, setting a positive example for constructive communication within your team.

In some situations, we're in Jane's place—we have an entire plan laid out, we've planned all the details, and we have a vision for what we want to accomplish. When the time comes to communicate your ideas, however, things take a turn. Between harsh colleagues and fumbled words, we fail to effectively convey our vision.

The path from simple ideas to a fully implemented plan is a deceptively difficult one. One of the most challenging aspects of this is getting others to understand what we want. As a result, assertive leadership relies heavily on communicating your ideas clearly, concisely, and effectively, especially to those who don't necessarily share your beliefs. To do this, assertive leaders must adopt techniques like:

1.   **Active Listening** – Ensuring that communication is a two-way street by fully engaging with others' responses and addressing concerns or questions to promote mutual understanding.

2.   **Clarification and Summarization** – Reiterating and summarizing key points during conversations to avoid misunderstandings and confirm that everyone is on the same page.

3.   **Non-verbal Communication** – Utilizing body language, eye contact, and tone of voice to reinforce the message and display confidence, helping others to trust and follow the leader's direction.

4.   **Adaptability in Communication Styles** – Adjusting the communication approach based on the audience, whether

formal, informal, detailed, or brief, depending on the group's needs and preferences.

5.   **Providing Concrete Examples** – Supporting abstract ideas with clear, relatable examples that make the vision tangible and easier to grasp.

6.   **Encouraging Feedback** – Creating an environment where others feel comfortable sharing their thoughts, which can lead to better refinement of ideas and overall improvement of the plan.

7.   **Patience and Repetition** – Understanding that not everyone will immediately understand complex ideas, so being willing to repeat and clarify information as necessary.

8.   **Framing Messages Positively** – Emphasizing the benefits and positive outcomes of the plan, especially for those who may be skeptical or resistant to change.

9.   **Setting Clear Expectations** – Clearly outlining roles, responsibilities, and the steps required to achieve the vision, ensuring that everyone knows their part in the larger goal.

10.   **Demonstrating Confidence and Consistency** – Showing unwavering belief in the plan while being consistent in messaging helps build trust and motivates others to follow through.

With all of these tools in your assertiveness toolkit, you can get your ideas across clearly while simultaneously reinforcing your leadership.

As a leader, it's important to recognize that you can't do everything by yourself. Rome wasn't built in a day, nor was it built by the emperor alone! In your quest to make your ideas a reality, you need to surround yourself with a good team that can steer you closer to success. Building an assertive team culture in the workplace is crucial for fostering a productive and positive work environment where individuals feel empowered to communicate openly and contribute effectively. Assertive team culture encourages team members to express their ideas, concerns, and feedback confidently and respectfully. This openness promotes innovation and problem-solving as diverse perspectives are considered, leading to more creative solutions and better decision-making processes.

Before you make your ideas a reality, you first have to set the tone by creating an assertive environment. As a leader, you'll automatically serve as a model for how others should act and communicate, but you'll also need to explicitly and intentionally create an environment that makes assertiveness the default communication style. To do this, there are several steps you can take, such as:

1.   **Lead by Example** – Demonstrate assertive behavior yourself by communicating clearly, confidently, and respectfully, showing others the standard to follow.

2.   **Establish Clear Communication Guidelines** – Set expectations for how communication should occur, emphasizing assertiveness, honesty, and respect in all interactions.

3.   **Encourage Open Dialogue** – Foster an environment where team members feel comfortable expressing their ideas and opinions without fear of being judged or dismissed.

4.   **Provide Assertiveness Training** – Offer workshops or training sessions that teach team members how to communicate assertively, helping them gain the skills to speak up and advocate for their needs.

5.   **Promote a Feedback Culture** – Encourage regular and constructive feedback, both giving and receiving, to help individuals improve their communication style and approach.

6.   **Recognize and Reward Assertive Behavior** – Publicly acknowledge and reward individuals who communicate assertively and effectively, reinforcing this as a desired behavior.

7.   **Address Passive or Aggressive Behavior** – Confront passive or aggressive communication styles immediately, explaining how assertiveness leads to more productive and respectful interactions.

8.   **Create a Safe Space for Conflict Resolution** – Teach and model assertive conflict resolution techniques, allowing team members to address disagreements calmly and constructively.

9.   **Provide Opportunities for Leadership** – Allow team members to take the lead on projects or meetings, giving them a chance to practice and develop their assertiveness in real situations.

10.   **Regularly Assess the Communication Climate** – Continuously monitor how communication is flowing within the team, addressing any gaps in assertiveness and adjusting your approach as necessary to maintain a strong, assertive environment.

Perhaps the most important aspect of creating an assertive team environment is making yourself available. The more people rely on you, your leadership, and your instruction, the more important it becomes to keep open lines of communication. With more leadership comes more responsibility—as much as your team members are working to bring your ideas to life, you are also working to make sure that everyone is as productive, comfortable, and communicative as they can be.

Now that we've taken a full deep dive into the world of assertiveness, it's time to tackle the last big aspect of this life skill: sustainability. In the next chapter, we'll talk about how to stoke the fire of assertiveness in the long term, as well as how to keep the flames alive for years to come.

Chapter 12:

Maintaining Long-Term

Assertiveness

A plan you have been working on for a long time is beginning to take shape.

No one can attest to the importance of habit formation more than Robert de Haan, a risk mitigation specialist and business consultant. In his 2019 account, he describes one particular boardroom of a notable company, surrounded by top executives. At first, the training session was like any other. He projected a sample phishing email and asked the executives to identify the red flags. Impressively, they all correctly spotted the phishing indicators. He praised them for being able to tell this risky email from all the others before springing a surprising truth on them. Before the meeting, de Haan had sent this exact email to all the people in the boardroom. All of them had clicked on the spam link embedded in the email.

It wasn't because the executives were incompetent or ignorant, de Haan explained. They had fallen prey to a potential security breach because, although they all knew what a phishing email looked like, they hadn't yet made it a habit to examine all of their emails for red flags. In the middle of a busy workday, even their own knowledge had failed.

In today's fast-paced business world, we're often overwhelmed with responsibilities, feeling time-pressured and distracted. This makes it hard to focus on every task, especially routine ones like checking emails. To combat this lapse in mindfulness, de Haan suggests that we "move the awareness thought process from a conscious process to a habitual process" (de Haan, 2019, p. 3). In short, we must identify important processes in our lives, and then turn them into habits.

Unlike deliberate actions, habits are managed by an impulsive processing system and require minimal conscious effort. This makes it easier to avoid phishing attempts. Developing a habit typically takes at least 21 to 28 days, and often up to 8 weeks, for a conscious practice to become automatic. Once established, these habits free up mental resources for more complex tasks.

What do phishing emails have to do with assertiveness? The same principle goes for communication—if you find yourself in the middle of a busy workday, or if you're not paying attention to how you're communicating, assertiveness can fly right out of the window. To create a lifelong skill, we have to take something we know a lot about and ingrain it into our daily routines. In short—assertiveness needs to become a habit.

Sustaining Assertiveness Over Time

In the words of James Clear, an expert on habit formation and author of *Atomic Habits*, "All big things come from small beginnings. The seed of every habit is a single, tiny decision. But as that decision is repeated, a habit sprouts and grows stronger" (Clear, 2018, p. 26).

Perhaps the most important thing you can do to make assertiveness into a habit is to start strong; that is, try to engage in one act of intentional assertiveness per day, at minimum. As difficult as it may be at first, the way you start your assertiveness journey will set the tone for all of your efforts moving forward. Luckily, you've already taken the first several steps—reading this book included! By consistently applying assertive behaviors, you reinforce neural pathways associated with assertiveness, making it a natural part of how you communicate and interact with others. In addition to getting a good start, there are three things to keep in mind when it comes to sustainable assertiveness:

1. **Make space for reflection.** Another key aspect of sustaining assertive behavior is self-awareness and reflection. Continuously assess your communication style and behaviors to identify areas where assertiveness can be strengthened or refined. Reflect on past

experiences to learn from successes and challenges, adjusting your approach as needed to achieve more effective outcomes in future interactions.

2. **Prioritize self-care and manage stress.** Assertiveness can be challenging in high-pressure or emotionally charged situations. Practicing stress-reduction techniques such as mindfulness, deep breathing, or physical exercise can help you stay grounded and composed. Taking care of your well-being ensures that you can approach interactions with clarity and confidence, sustaining assertive behavior consistently.

3. **Seek support and feedback.** Surround yourself with positive influences who value assertive communication and can offer constructive advice for navigating challenging situations. By cultivating a supportive network and practicing assertiveness consistently, you can sustain this valuable skill over the long term, enhancing your personal and professional relationships while achieving greater confidence and success.

All three of these things can be adopted into your lifestyle by adding them to your calendar—literally. Whether you use a digital calendar or a physical planner, making space for sustainable assertiveness practices is something that you should actively pursue. As silly as it might sound, getting everything in writing is another important part of reinforcing your assertiveness into a habit. Sticky notes, calendar events, and phone notifications are all great ways of encouraging your future self to keep going.

Adapting to Changing Circumstances

As was covered back in Chapter 1, there's no handbook for how to communicate effectively. There's also no blanket solution or universal mold for how assertiveness should be practiced. This is especially important to remember as you consider the future, particularly as you grow older and engage with different groups of people.

In early adulthood, assertive communication is crucial for navigating the complexities of higher education, career beginnings, and personal relationships. Young adults often face significant transitions, such as starting college or entering the workforce, where clear and confident communication can set the tone for future success. Being able to assertively negotiate salaries, set boundaries with colleagues, and express expectations in romantic relationships helps young adults establish a balanced and fulfilling life. This stage involves refining the ability to communicate needs and boundaries without aggression or passivity, thus fostering professional growth and personal well-being.

As individuals progress into midlife, assertive communication becomes essential in managing more complex life roles, including career advancement, parenting, and caring for aging parents. This stage often requires balancing multiple responsibilities, making it vital to communicate needs and limits effectively. Assertive communication helps in advocating for oneself at work, setting boundaries with children, and negotiating caregiving duties within the family. This period also involves modeling assertive behavior for the next generation, demonstrating the importance of clear, respectful communication in maintaining healthy relationships and achieving personal goals.

In later life, assertive communication continues to play a vital role in maintaining independence and ensuring quality of life. Older adults may need to assert their preferences in healthcare decisions, manage changing family dynamics, and navigate retirement. Communicating assertively helps them express their wishes and maintain autonomy, fostering a sense of control and dignity. Additionally, assertive communication can help older adults remain socially connected, addressing issues like loneliness and isolation by encouraging open and honest interactions with friends, family, and caregivers.

By mastering assertive communication at each stage, individuals can build stronger relationships, achieve personal and professional goals, and navigate life's challenges with confidence and resilience.

Resources for Further Growth in Assertiveness

When we think of therapy, we might think of mental health issues like depression and anxiety, or we could consider the dozens of old Hollywood portrayals of shrinks and mental illness. This is an inherently flawed view—nothing needs to be wrong for us to seek mental health counseling and help. In fact, according to Statista, about 55.8 million American adults sought mental health counseling of some sort over the course of one year (Vankar, 2024).

Therapists don't just deal with crises. As trained professionals, therapists and psychiatrists are academics, researchers, and industry experts who can help us better understand ourselves, our behaviors, and our underlying beliefs. Luckily, the stigma around mental health assistance is waning, and seeking therapy is no longer a cut-and-dry sign of weakness or personal failings. Rather, it's both a means of dealing with issues we face, as well as acting as a preventative mental health measure.

Contrary to the image that has historically been portrayed by movies and shows—a patient sitting dramatically on a chaise lounge as they monologue to an emotionless therapist—there are many different kinds of therapy.

1. **Cognitive Behavioral Therapy (CBT):** CBT is a widely used therapy that focuses on identifying and changing negative thought patterns and behaviors. It is based on the premise that our thoughts influence our feelings and behaviors, and aims to teach clients practical skills to manage their emotions and improve their coping strategies.

2. **Psychodynamic Therapy:** Rooted in Freudian principles, psychodynamic therapy explores how unconscious thoughts and past experiences influence current behaviors and relationships. It aims to uncover unresolved conflicts and unconscious processes to promote insight and self-awareness.

3. **Humanistic Therapy:** Humanistic therapy, including approaches like Person-Centered Therapy (Carl Rogers) and Gestalt Therapy (Fritz Perls), emphasizes personal growth, self-acceptance, and the belief that individuals have the capacity for self-direction and realization of their potential. It focuses on the present moment, the client's subjective experience, and the therapeutic relationship.

4. **Interpersonal Therapy (IPT):** IPT is a time-limited therapy that focuses on improving interpersonal relationships and communication skills. It addresses specific interpersonal issues such as grief, role transitions, interpersonal conflicts, and social isolation.

5. **Behavioral Therapy:** Behavioral therapies, including techniques such as Exposure Therapy, Behavior Modification, and Dialectical Behavior Therapy (DBT), focus on modifying behaviors through reinforcement, conditioning, and skills training. These therapies are often used to treat phobias, anxiety disorders, and substance abuse.

6. **Mindfulness-Based Therapies:** Therapies such as Mindfulness-Based Stress Reduction (MBSR) and Mindfulness-Based Cognitive Therapy (MBCT) integrate mindfulness practices with cognitive and behavioral techniques to promote self-awareness, stress reduction, and emotional regulation.

7. **Eclectic or Integrative Therapy:** Many therapists use an eclectic approach, combining techniques from different therapeutic modalities to tailor treatment to the individual needs of clients. This integrative approach may draw on elements of CBT, psychodynamic therapy, humanistic principles, and other therapeutic approaches.

These therapies vary in their theoretical foundations, techniques, and goals, but they share the common objective of promoting mental health, personal growth, and well-being. The choice of therapy depends on your specific situation, preferences, and therapeutic goals, and may involve collaboration between you and your therapist to determine the most effective approach.

While you should always consult your doctor or licensed therapist for medical advice, some of the most effective forms of therapy for building and sustaining assertiveness are cognitive-behavioral therapy, interpersonal therapy, and mindfulness-based therapies. Most of the time, however, therapists are trained in a variety of schools, and one therapist may be able to offer several different methods based on what you need to grow your assertiveness.

In the context of assertiveness and communication, seeing a mental health professional will allow you to have a more structured game plan for improving your self-esteem and assertiveness, possibly more than you could do alone. Therapy will also keep you accountable and allow you to complete regular (and less avoidable) check-ins, letting you keep track of your progress over time.

Outside of the logistical side of things, it's also important to see your therapist as a resource. In addition to adjusting your mindset and behaviors, they'll also be able to provide you with additional resources like books, worksheets, and methods that you might not find anywhere else.

If therapy doesn't sound appealing to you, or if circumstances prevent you from seeing a therapist regularly, workshops and classes are a great alternative. Like therapy, workshops and classes can offer structured learning experiences focused on specific topics or skills that you might want to focus on as you grow. They provide several benefits:

1. **Education and Skill Acquisition:** Workshops and classes offer opportunities to learn new knowledge, techniques, and practical skills. Whether it's a workshop on assertiveness training, a cooking class, or a financial planning seminar, participants gain valuable insights and expertise.

2. **Hands-On Learning:** Many workshops and classes involve hands-on activities, simulations, or group exercises that facilitate experiential learning. This active engagement helps participants internalize concepts and apply them in real-life situations.

3. **Community and Networking:** Workshops and classes often bring together like-minded individuals who share common interests or goals. Participants can network, exchange ideas, and build supportive relationships with others in their field or community.

4. **Personal Growth and Confidence:** Engaging in workshops and classes can boost self-esteem and confidence in and of themselves, namely by challenging

individuals to step outside their comfort zones and acquire new skills. Achieving mastery or competency in a new area fosters a sense of accomplishment and personal growth.

Therapy, workshops, and classes offer diverse benefits that contribute to holistic personal development, emotional well-being, and skill enhancement. Whether seeking therapeutic support for emotional healing, attending workshops to learn new skills, or participating in classes for ongoing education, these opportunities play integral roles in fostering growth, resilience, and fulfillment in individuals' lives.

Preventing Assertiveness From Slipping into Aggression

I didn't watch the Pixar film *Inside Out* until I babysat one of my friend's young children. The film follows Riley, a young girl whose family has just moved across the country to a brand-new city. We see Riley's experiences through the characters who live in her head, with each character representing an emotion. As far as kids' movies go, *Inside Out* provides a colorful glimpse into the mental health of people of all ages.

I was particularly intrigued by the film's portrayal of Anger, especially during scenes when Anger interacted with the other emotions. At some point during our watch party, I realized something fascinating—Anger only turned into aggression when a problem in Riley's experience went unaddressed. While *Inside Out* may not be to everyone's liking as a movie, it does provide an interesting insight into what our anger can tell us.

For our purposes, we can think of anger as a canary in a coal mine. In other words, anger is a sign that something is amiss in our lives, whether it's an unmet need or a specific interaction that leaves us feeling poorly. The difference between assertive behavior and aggressive behavior is the point at which we address the problems that make us angry.

With this in mind, the first step in catching aggressiveness before it develops is to work on your emotional intelligence and self-awareness. Building awareness in a meaningful way will let you hear the canary more clearly, so to speak. It will help you stop your anger in its tracks.

This can be easier said than done, however, especially if you tend to lean more toward an aggressive communication style. While you can try to stop aggressive behavior by using the techniques that we've been talking about, you ultimately won't be able to quash aggression until you deal with the underlying anger (and root problems) that lie beneath.

Effective anger management techniques can help individuals handle their emotions constructively and avoid the negative consequences of uncontrolled anger. Here are several strategies for managing anger:

1. **Recognize early signs:** Be aware of the physical and emotional signs of anger, such as a racing heart, clenched fists, or irritability. Recognizing these signs early can help you address anger before it escalates.

2. **Practice deep breathing:** Use deep breathing exercises to calm your physiological response to anger. Inhale slowly through your nose, hold for a few seconds, and exhale slowly through your mouth. This can help reduce tension and bring your focus back to a more controlled state.

3. **Take a timeout:** Remove yourself from the situation that is triggering your anger. A short break or a walk can help you cool down and gain perspective, allowing you to approach the situation with a clearer mind.

4. **Use relaxation techniques:** Engage in activities that help you relax, such as progressive muscle relaxation, meditation, or visualization. These techniques can reduce overall stress and make it easier to manage anger when it arises.

5. **Problem-solving:** Focus your efforts on finding constructive solutions to the issue at hand. Identifying the root cause of your anger and working toward a resolution can help prevent future conflicts and reduce feelings of frustration.

6. **Practice physical and mental self-care:** Physical activity can help reduce stress and improve your mood. Regular exercise helps to release built-up tension and promotes overall emotional well-being. Engage in activities that allow you to express your emotions in a positive way, such as journaling, art, or hobbies. These outlets can provide a constructive release for pent-up emotions.

7. **Seek support:** As we've mentioned before, it can make a world of difference when you talk to friends, family, or a counselor about your feelings. The same goes for anger. Sometimes, discussing your emotions with others can provide new perspectives and coping strategies.

8. **Reflect on triggers:** Analyze the situations or patterns that commonly trigger your anger. Understanding these triggers can help you anticipate and manage your responses more effectively in the future.

While you might not catch your anger every time it creeps up, your awareness of the potential for aggression makes you all the more ready to tackle aggression as it arises. In combination with these techniques, you'll find that keeping aggressive communication at bay will reinforce your assertiveness in a meaningful, sustainable way.

Over the past 12 chapters, we've learned a lot about assertiveness and the amazing outcomes it can bring us when used correctly. We've explored all of the tips, techniques, and methods that can carry us to our goals and beyond, and we've looked at countless cases in which assertive communication was vital. In the next chapter, we'll tie it all together and recap the most essential parts of assertiveness.

Conclusion

The journey of learning assertiveness is a transformative path toward personal empowerment and enriched interpersonal relationships. Throughout this book, we have explored the fundamental principles, practical strategies, and psychological insights that underpin assertive communication, including:

- assertive communication in the context of other communication methods

- the foundational elements for assertiveness, self-awareness, and self-esteem

- the observable displays of assertiveness through both verbal and non-verbal techniques

- assertiveness in common situations like handling criticism and feedback, saying "no," and negotiating

- assertiveness in social, personal, and professional settings

- overcoming cultural and psychological barriers to assertiveness

- daily assertiveness practices like journaling and role-playing

- the importance of emotional intelligence in assertiveness

- skills like positive language and conflict resolution

- leading with assertiveness and building an assertive team culture

- building long-term assertiveness and the importance of habit formation

Assertiveness is not merely a skill but a mindset that empowers individuals to navigate life's complexities with clarity and integrity. It involves self-awareness, where individuals recognize their emotions, values, and beliefs, and learn to communicate them authentically. This self-awareness forms the foundation for assertive behavior, enabling individuals to express themselves confidently while considering the perspectives and feelings of others.

Throughout this journey, you, dear readers, have been encouraged to practice and integrate assertive behaviors into your daily lives. From assertive body language and tone of voice to active listening and conflict resolution, each aspect contributes to building stronger and more meaningful connections with others. By cultivating assertiveness, individuals not only enhance their well-being but also contribute positively to their professional environments, fostering collaborative teamwork and effective leadership.

Moreover, the benefits of assertiveness extend beyond individual growth to impact broader societal dynamics. In workplaces, assertive communication promotes a culture of respect, innovation, and inclusivity, where diverse perspectives are valued and creativity thrives. In personal relationships, assertiveness nurtures mutual understanding and trust, laying the groundwork for healthier and more fulfilling connections.

As you conclude your journey with this book, you will find that you are now equipped with practical tools and a deeper understanding of assertiveness as a lifelong practice. The path to mastering assertive communication requires ongoing reflection, adaptation, and commitment to personal growth. By continuing to apply the principles and techniques explored here, you can navigate future challenges with confidence and resilience, fostering a life characterized by authenticity, respect, and meaningful communication.

In closing, learning assertiveness is not just about acquiring a skill but embracing a mindset that empowers individuals to assert their rights, express their needs, and cultivate harmonious relationships. May this book serve as a valuable resource and inspiration on your journey toward greater self-confidence, effective communication, and personal fulfillment through assertiveness.

Glossary

- **Accommodating conflict style (passive-aggressive)**: This style involves putting others' needs ahead of one's own while suppressing personal grievances. Accommodators may comply outwardly but harbor resentment.

- **Aggression**: A communication style characterized by frustration, anger, and other negative emotions, which entails a high preference for communication and a low level of conscientiousness toward others.

- **Assertiveness**: A life skill that entails self-demonstration through a logical series of details and facts that describe who you are to others. A way of effectively connecting yourself with the world around you. A communication style that incorporates both a high preference for communication and a high level of conscientiousness toward others.

- **Avoidant conflict style (passive)**: People with this style sidestep conflicts and prefer to withdraw from disagreements. They often avoid addressing the underlying issues. To engage with avoiders, create a safe and supportive environment, gently encouraging them to share their thoughts and concerns. Emphasize the importance of resolving the issue for mutual benefit.

- **Boundaries**: The guidelines, limits, or rules that a person establishes to define permissible behavior, interactions, and expectations in relationships, both personal and professional.

- **Collaborating conflict style (assertive-assertive):** Collaborative individuals seek win-win solutions by engaging in open dialogue and mutual problem-solving. They aim to satisfy both parties' needs. To work effectively with collaborators, foster an environment of trust and cooperation. Encourage brainstorming and creative thinking to find solutions that benefit everyone involved.

- **Competing conflict style (assertive-aggressive):** This style involves asserting one's own needs and goals at the expense of others. Individuals using this approach prioritize winning the conflict over maintaining relationships. To deal with this style, it's important to stay calm and assertive, clearly stating your own needs while seeking common ground. Focus on collaborative problem-solving to find mutually beneficial solutions.

- **Compromising conflict style (assertive-yielding):** Compromisers aim to find a middle ground by negotiating and making concessions. They seek quick resolutions that partially satisfy both parties. When dealing with compromisers, focus on clear communication and fairness. Acknowledge their willingness to find a balanced solution and work together to reach an agreement that addresses the most important needs of both sides.

- **Diversity, equity, and inclusion (DEI):** An acronym describing the initiatives companies make to give marginalized communities equal opportunities to make meaningful decisions and occupy leadership positions.

- **Emotional intelligence (EI):** The ability to recognize, understand, and manage one's own emotions, as well as to recognize, understand, and influence the emotions of others.

- **External locus of control:** The belief that external factors determine the outcomes of events in one's life. Individuals with a strong external locus of control feel that they have limited influence over what happens to them and often attribute success or failure to outside forces beyond their control.

- **External self-awareness:** The extent to which we can see ourselves from the perspectives of others, specifically in social, professional, and otherwise interpersonal situations.

- **Inner voice:** Also known as self-talk, inner voice refers to the internal self-directed thoughts that individuals experience within their minds. It includes the thoughts, beliefs, judgments, and interpretations that people have about themselves, others, and the world around them.

- **Internal locus of control:** The belief that one can influence the outcomes of their actions and events in their life through their efforts, decisions, and abilities. Individuals with a strong internal locus of control feel empowered and accountable, attributing success and failure to their own actions rather than external factors or chance.

- **Internal self-awareness:** The extent of the clarity with which we know ourselves, our wants, our needs, and our preferences.

- **Label:** A descriptive term or category assigned to a person, group, or behavior based on certain characteristics, traits, or attributes. Labels can be positive or negative and may influence perceptions, attitudes, and behaviors toward individuals or groups. Labels are used to classify and understand individuals within social, cultural, or psychological contexts, but they can also oversimplify complex identities or experiences, potentially leading to stereotyping or stigmatization.

- **Passive-aggression:** A communication style characterized by negative emotions that entails a low preference for communication and a low level of conscientiousness toward others.

- **Passivity:** A communication style characterized by a low preference for communication but a high level of conscientiousness toward others, often called shyness or reservedness.

- **Positive language:** Communication that emphasizes constructive and optimistic words and phrases to convey ideas, express emotions, or interact with others.

- **Rumination:** Cyclical negative thinking that prompts negative feelings about life, specifically triggered by past events.

- **Self-awareness:** The overall evaluation of one's worth or value, which can be objective or subjective, and which is usually based on previous life experiences or ongoing social feedback.

- **Self-care:** The practice of taking deliberate actions to maintain and improve one's physical, mental, and emotional well-being. It involves activities and habits that reduce stress, promote health, and enhance overall quality of life, such as exercising, eating healthily, getting enough sleep, and engaging in hobbies or relaxation techniques.

- **Self-esteem:** The subjective evaluation of one's worth, value, or significance. It reflects the overall opinion and perception an individual holds about themselves, encompassing feelings of self-worth, self-respect, and self-acceptance. Self-esteem influences how individuals perceive their abilities, qualities, and achievements, shaping their confidence levels and behaviors in various aspects of life.

- **Social anxiety:** A mental health condition characterized by an intense fear of social situations and being judged or negatively evaluated by others. This fear can lead to significant distress and avoidance of social interactions, impacting daily activities, relationships, and overall quality of life.

Resources for Further Reading

- Alberti, R. E., & Emmons, M. L. (2017). *Your perfect right : assertiveness and equality in your life and relationships.* Impact Publishers, An Imprint Of New Harbinger Publications, Inc. ISBN: 9781626259607

- Aziz Gazipura. (2017). *Not nice : stop people pleasing, staying silent, & feeling guilty ... and start speaking up, saying no, asking boldly, and unapologetically being yourself.* B.C. Allen Publishing & Tonic Books. ISBN: 9780988979871

- Banks, R. (2020). *The Keys to Being Brilliantly Confident and More Assertive.* ISBN: 9781736274002

- Bower, S. (2004). *Asserting yourself: A Practical Guide For Positive Change.* Da Capo Press. ISBN: 9780201008371

- Cloud, H., & John Sims Townsend. (1995). *Boundaries. Workbook : when to say yes, when to say no to take control of your life.* Zondervan Pub. House. ISBN: 9780310494812

- Dale, P. (2021). *Did you say something, Susan? : how any woman can gain confidence with assertive communication.* ISBN: 9781098352202

- Hill, C. (2021). *Assertiveness Training: How to Stand Up for Yourself, Boost Your Confidence, and Improve Assertive Communication Skills.* Mindful Happiness. ISBN: 9781087902852

- King, P. (2018). *The art of everyday assertiveness: Speak up. Say no. Set boundaries. Take back control.* ISBN: 9781983449437

- Murphy, J. (2011). *Assertiveness : how to stand up for yourself and still win the respect of others.* ISBN: 9781495446856

- Paterson, R. J. (2000). *Assertiveness workbook - how to express your ideas and stand up for yourself at work and in relationships.* New Harbinger Publications, U.S. ISBN: 9781572242098

- Patterson, K., Grenny, J., Switzler, A., & Mcmillan, R. (2012). *Crucial conversations : tools for talking when the stakes are high.* Mcgraw-Hill. ISBN: 9780071771320

- Potts, C., & Potts, S. (2013). *Assertiveness : how to be strong in every situation.* Mjf Books. ISBN: 9781606712221

- Smith, M. J. (2011). *When I Say No, I Feel Guilty: How to Cope, Using the Skills of Systematic Assertive Therapy.* Random House Publishing Group. ISBN: 9780307785442

- Stone, D., & Heen, S. (2015). *Thanks for the feedback : the science and art of receiving feedback well : (even when it is off base, unfair, poorly delivered, and frankly, you're not in the mood).* Portfolio Penguin. ISBN: 9780670922635

- Ury, W. (2007). *The Power of a Positive No: How to Say NO and Still Get a YES.* Bantam. ISBN: 9780553903522

Exercises and Worksheets

Every Person's Bill of Rights

If you Google the words "personal bill of rights" you'll either find a transcription of the United States Bill of Rights, or you'll find a list of self-affirming phrases and mantras aimed at reinforcing your assertiveness. For our purposes, we'll be looking at the second set of search results today.

The Bill of Assertive Rights consists of a series of statements that emphasize our freedom to express ourselves authentically without disrespecting others. These 10 choices represent fundamental rights we all possess, similar to other inherent rights, and they outline what we are entitled to.

These statements help us recognize when and how we can be more assertive and guide us in responding to others who are not assertive with us. They also highlight that we have the right to choose not to be assertive if we prefer, though we must accept the consequences of that choice.

In his book *When I Say No, I Feel Guilty*, Manuel J. Smith introduced the 10-point "Bill of Assertive Rights." These rights are centered around one key principle: The right to be the final judge of yourself is the prime assertive right, allowing no one to manipulate you. Nowadays, you'll find myriad different versions of this idea, some as long as 100 bullet points! Here, we'll look at some of the most commonly found phrases:

1. The right to be treated with respect.

2. The right to have and express your feelings and opinions.

3. The right to be listened to and taken seriously.

4. The right to set your priorities.

5. The right to say "no" without feeling guilty.

6. The right to get what you pay for.

7. The right to make mistakes.

8. The right to choose not to assert yourself.

To center yourself at some point in your daily life, consider the Bill of Assertive Rights. For some, this might be best done if written down and placed somewhere you'll see it often, like your desk or your fridge. For others, it may be better to set the list as your phone background so that you can carry it with you wherever you go. No matter your method, take a few moments every day to remember your rights.

Ranking Exercise for Thinking Traps

Rate the questions below as either a 1 (I never think this way), 2 (I sometimes think this way), or 3 (I always think this way). After you've given your answers, look over the results section.

For each thinking trap in the results section, navigate to the corresponding questions and tally up the ratings you provided. Do this for each of the thinking traps. Your biggest thinking traps will be those with the highest numbers.

Questions

1. _ I need others to approve of me to feel that I am worth something.

2. _ I feel like a fortune teller, predicting bad things will happen to me.

3. _ I believe others think about me in a negative way.

4. _ I tend to discount the good things about me.

5. _ I either like a person or do not, there is no in-between for me.

6. _ I minimize the importance of serious situations.

7. _ I compare myself to others.

8. _ I amplify things well beyond their real importance in life.

9. _ I act as if I have a crystal ball, forecasting negative events in my life.

10. _ What others think about me is more important than what I think about myself.

11. _ It doesn't matter what my choices are, they always fall flat.

12. _ I make decisions based on my feelings.

13. _ I draw conclusions without carefully reviewing the necessary details.

14. _ If a problem develops in my life, you can bet it has something to do with the way I am.

15. _ To feel good, I need others to recognize me.

16. _ I must have things my way in my life.

17. _ I tend to blame myself for bad things.

18. _ Without even asking, I think other people see me in a negative light.

19. _ I do few things as well as others.

20. _ I hold myself responsible for things that are beyond my control.

21. _ I tend to not emphasize the positive traits I have.

22. _ Things seem to go all right or all wrong in my world.

23. _ I tend to pick out negative details in a situation and dwell on them.

24. _ I tend to exaggerate the importance of minor events.

25. _ I have a habit of predicting that things will go wrong in any given situation.

26. _ I have a lot of "shoulds," "oughts," and "musts" in my life.

27. _ I downplay my accomplishments.

28. _ I have been known to make a mountain out of a molehill.

29. _ Most people are better at things than I am.

30. _ When a new rule comes out at school, work, or home, I think it must have been made because of something I did.

31. _ When faced with several possible outcomes, I tend to think the worst is going to happen.

32. _ Things ought to be a certain way.

33. _ If I feel a certain way about something, I am usually right.

34. _ In my mind, things are either black or white, there are no gray areas.

35. _ People only say nice things to me because they want something or because they are trying to flatter me.

36. _ I tend to minimize the consequences of my actions, especially if they result in negative outcomes.

37. _ I jump to conclusions without considering alternative points of view.

38. _ If people ignore me, I think they have negative thoughts about me.

39. _ My feelings reflect the way things are.

40. _ When something negative happens, it is just terrible.

41. _ I tend to dwell on the things I do not like about myself.

42. _ I tend to filter out the positives in a situation and focus more on the negatives.

Results

- **Externalization of Self-Worth** (1, 10, 15): Total _

The development and maintenance of your self-worth are based almost exclusively on how the external world views you.

- **Fortune Telling** (2, 9, 25): Total _

The process of foretelling or predicting the negative outcome of a future event or events and believing this prediction is true for you.

- **Mind Reading** (3, 18, 38): Total _

One's conclusion is that someone is reacting negatively or thinking negatively about them without specific evidence to support that conclusion.

- **Disqualify the Positive** (4, 21, 35): Total _

The process of rejecting or discounting positive experiences, traits, or attributes.

- **Black-and-White Thinking** (5, 22, 34): Total _

The tendency to view all experiences as fitting into one of two categories (e.g., positive or negative; good or bad) without the ability to place oneself, others, and experiences along a continuum.

- **Minimization** (6, 27, 36): Total _

The process of minimizing or discounting the importance of some event, trait, or circumstance.

- **Comparison** (7, 19, 29): Total _

The tendency to compare oneself whereby the outcome typically results in the conclusion that one is inferior or worse off than others.

- **Magnification** (8, 24, 28): Total _

The tendency to exaggerate or magnify either the positive or negative importance or consequence of some personal trait, event, or circumstance.

- **Over-Generalization** (11, 14, 40): Total _

The process of formulating rules or conclusions based on limited experience and applying these rules across broad and unrelated situations.

- **Emotional Reasoning** (12, 33, 39): Total _

The predominant use of an emotional state to form conclusions about oneself, others, or situations.

- **Jumping to Conclusions** (13, 31, 37): Total _

The process of drawing a negative conclusion in the absence of specific evidence to support that conclusion.

- **Selective Abstractions** (23, 41, 42): Total _

The process of exclusively focusing on one negative aspect or detail of a situation and magnifying the importance of that detail, thereby casting the whole situation in a negative context.

- **Should Statements** (16, 26, 32): Total _

The process of applying personal standards of behavior, standards for other people, or standards about the way the world functions to all situations. Involves the use of words like "should," "ought," and "must."

- **Personalization** (17, 20, 30): Total _

The process of assuming personal causality for situations, events, and reactions of others when there is no evidence supporting that conclusion.

Writing Exercise

1. We all fall into thinking traps from time to time. What were your top three thinking traps?

2. How do you think these thinking traps may inhibit the following:

   A. Your performance?

   B. Your long-term goals?

   C. Your relationships?

3. For each of your top three thinking traps, come up with a strategy that will allow you to think more realistically and effectively in the future.

   A. Thinking trap 1:

   B. Thinking trap 2:

   C. Thinking trap 3:

Identifying Communication Styles Worksheet

For each example, think about how a person would respond if they used each communication style. Your responses should look something like this:

You're rushing to get ready for work one morning when your doorbell rings. It's one of your friends. They ask if you want to go to brunch at a new restaurant downtown. This clearly isn't urgent, but they're asking anyway even though they know your work schedule.

Passive	"Okay, I guess I could use my PTO to call in sick today."
Aggressive	"Are you blind? Why would I want to have lunch with you when I'm clearly busy?"
Assertive	"I'm in the office today, so I can't meet up right now. I'll send you my availability for next week so you know when I'm free. Let's plan a brunch for next week!"

- Your friend asks to borrow your car, but this will be a major inconvenience for you.

Passive	
Aggressive	
Assertive	

- Your manager asks you to stay late at the end of a long workday, even though you already told them that you had evening plans.

Passive	
Aggressive	
Assertive	

- Your spouse/partner didn't wash the dishes even though they said they would, and you're too busy to do housework right now.

Passive	
Aggressive	
Assertive	

Assertiveness Baseline Assessment

For each of the following locations, feelings, people, and other areas of your life, rank how assertive you typically feel when presented with these situations. For each bullet point, mark each situation with a 1 (I am rarely or never assertive in this situation), 2 (I am sometimes assertive but not usually), or 3 (I am usually assertive in this situation). Complete this baseline assessment every month and keep track of what answers change or improve. If the location or people are not applicable, skip this number.

Locations

1. Home _

2. Career _

3. School _

4. Socially _

5. Place of worship _

People

1. Intimate friends/partners _

2. Strangers _

3. Aggressive communicators _

4. Angry people _

5. Timid people _

6. Men _

7. Women _

8. Authority figures _

9. Children _

Feelings

1. Anger _

2. Sadness _

3. Happiness _

4. Love _

5. Fear _

6. Self-doubt _

7. Positive self-statements _

Other Areas

1. Making requests _

2. Saying "no" _

3. Giving compliments _

4. Receiving compliments _

5. Giving criticism _

6. Receiving criticism _

7. Making conversation _

Specific Personal Assertiveness Goals for the Month

SMART habits are a structured approach to developing behaviors that lead to specific and achievable goals. Each letter in SMART—Specific, Measurable, Achievable, Relevant, and Time-bound—guides the process of setting and maintaining effective habits. As you make your goals for the month, go down the SMART checklist and make sure that your goals fit the criteria. SMART habits are:

- **Specific**. They define exactly what needs to be accomplished. For example, rather than setting a vague goal like "exercise more," a specific habit might be "go for a 30-minute jog every morning before work." This clarity helps in focusing efforts and understanding the exact actions required.

- **Measurable**. They include criteria for tracking progress and determining success. Measurable habits allow individuals to monitor their advancement over time. For instance, tracking the number of jogs completed each week provides tangible evidence of progress and motivates continued effort.

- **Achievable**. They are realistic and attainable within the resources and constraints available. Setting goals that are too ambitious can lead to frustration and burnout. Instead, SMART habits encourage setting targets that are challenging yet feasible with dedication and perseverance.

- **Relevant**. They are meaningful and aligned with broader personal or professional objectives. A relevant habit connects directly to desired outcomes, ensuring that efforts contribute to overall success and fulfillment.

- **Time-bound**. They have a specific timeframe or deadline for completion. This component creates urgency and helps prioritize tasks effectively. For example, committing to completing a certain number of jogs within a month provides a clear timeline for achieving fitness goals.

By applying the SMART criteria, individuals can develop habits that are clear, measurable, achievable, relevant, and time-bound. This structured approach enhances motivation, accountability, and focus, leading to more effective behavior change and sustained progress toward desired outcomes. Whether aiming for personal growth, health improvement, or professional success, SMART habits provide a systematic framework for turning intentions into actions and goals into achievements.

1. Goal One:

2. Goal Two:

3. Goal Three:

4. Goal Four:

Assertiveness Visualization Exercise

Visualization exercises offer profound psychological benefits by harnessing the power of imagination to positively influence thoughts, emotions, and behaviors. At its core, visualization involves creating detailed mental images or scenarios that evoke specific sensations and emotions. Through regular practice, individuals can experience a range of psychological benefits that enhance their overall well-being and performance in various aspects of life.

One significant benefit of visualization exercises is stress reduction. By immersing oneself in a calming and positive mental imagery, such as a peaceful beach or a serene forest, individuals can lower their cortisol levels and induce a relaxation response. This helps alleviate tension, anxiety, and even symptoms of depression, promoting a sense of inner peace and emotional stability.

Moreover, visualization exercises strengthen cognitive functions such as focus, concentration, and mental clarity. When visualizing specific goals, tasks, or challenges, individuals engage the brain's neural pathways associated with problem-solving and planning. This mental rehearsal primes the mind for success by enhancing motivation, improving decision-making skills, and boosting self-confidence.

Additionally, visualization exercises cultivate resilience and optimism by fostering a proactive mindset. By visualizing themselves overcoming obstacles or achieving desired outcomes, individuals develop a sense of control and agency over their circumstances. This positive outlook can buffer against setbacks, increase resilience in the face of adversity, and enhance overall psychological resilience.

Furthermore, visualization exercises can enhance skill acquisition and performance. Athletes, performers, and professionals often use visualization to mentally rehearse movements, strategies, or presentations. This mental practice primes the body and mind for optimal performance, improving muscle memory, coordination, and execution of complex tasks.

In conclusion, visualization exercises offer a powerful tool for harnessing the mind-body connection to promote mental well-being, enhance performance, and cultivate resilience. Whether used for relaxation, goal-setting, skill development, or overcoming challenges, regular practice of visualization can significantly impact psychological health by fostering positive emotions, improving cognitive functions, and empowering individuals to achieve their full potential.

This visualization technique uses four steps:

1. **Preparation:** Find a quiet and comfortable space where you can relax without distractions. Sit or lie down in a comfortable position and take a few deep breaths to relax your body and mind.

2. **Visualization Script:** Imagine yourself in a situation where you typically struggle with assertiveness, such as expressing your opinion in a meeting or setting boundaries with a friend. Visualize the scenario vividly: See the room around you, hear the voices and sounds, and feel the emotions you might typically experience in that situation. Now, envision yourself standing tall and feeling confident. Visualize a bright light surrounding you, filling you with a sense of calm and inner strength. See yourself speaking assertively and clearly. Hear your voice expressing your thoughts and feelings with confidence and conviction. Visualize the reactions of others as positive and respectful. See them nodding in agreement or acknowledging your perspective. Feel the sense of empowerment and satisfaction that comes with being assertive. Embrace the feeling of having successfully communicated your needs or opinions effectively.

3. **Reflection:** Take a moment to reflect on how you felt during the visualization exercise. Notice any sensations, emotions, or thoughts that arose. Consider how you can apply the feelings of confidence and assertiveness from the visualization to real-life situations. Visualize yourself using assertive communication in future scenarios, reinforcing the belief that you can express yourself confidently.

4. **Closing:** When you are ready, slowly bring your awareness back to the present moment. Take a few more deep breaths to ground yourself. Carry the feelings of empowerment and assertiveness with you as

you go about your day, knowing that you have practiced and strengthened your ability to assert yourself effectively.

If you want to listen to the visualization script instead of reading it during the exercise, navigate to text-to-speech software. Alternatively, you can copy the script into your smartphone's notes app and then navigate to the note settings for a built-in text-to-speech dictation.

Journaling Prompts

Regular journaling offers numerous benefits that contribute to overall mental, emotional, and even physical well-being. At its core, journaling provides a private and structured space for individuals to reflect, process thoughts, and explore their innermost feelings. This reflective practice allows people to gain clarity and insight into their experiences, helping them to understand themselves better and navigate life's challenges more effectively.

One of the key benefits of journaling is its therapeutic effect on mental health. Writing down thoughts and emotions can serve as a form of self-expression and emotional release. It allows individuals to externalize their concerns, worries, and anxieties, which can reduce stress levels and promote a sense of calmness and relaxation. This process can be particularly beneficial during times of heightened emotions or when facing difficult decisions or transitions in life.

Moreover, journaling helps to improve self-awareness. By documenting daily experiences, interactions, and reactions, individuals can identify recurring patterns of behavior or thought that may be influencing their lives. This self-awareness is crucial for personal growth and development, as it enables individuals to recognize strengths, areas for improvement, and opportunities for change.

Journaling also enhances problem-solving and decision-making skills. Through writing, individuals can analyze situations objectively, consider different perspectives, and weigh options more effectively. This structured reflection fosters critical thinking and creativity, empowering individuals to make informed choices and take proactive steps toward their goals.

Additionally, regular journaling supports goal-setting and achievement. By documenting aspirations, progress, and setbacks, individuals can track their growth over time and stay motivated toward achieving their desired outcomes. Journaling serves as a personal accountability tool, encouraging consistent action and commitment to personal and professional goals.

In the context of assertiveness, regular journaling provides an outlet for frustrations, a place for brainstorming, and a place to explore different perspectives. The next time you pull out your growth journal, try a couple of these assertiveness-focused prompts:

1. Write about a time when you successfully stood up for yourself. How did assertiveness play a role in the outcome?

2. Describe a situation where you struggled to be assertive. What were the challenges, and how did you overcome them?

3. Imagine yourself in a scenario where you need to assertively negotiate for a higher salary or better terms. How would you prepare for this conversation?

4. Write a dialogue between two characters—one who is assertive and one who is passive-aggressive—discussing a conflict. How does each approach impact the resolution?

5. Reflect on the difference between assertiveness and aggression. How can you ensure your communication style remains assertive in challenging situations?

6. Describe a workplace environment where assertive communication is valued. How does this contribute to productivity and team dynamics?

7. Write a letter to a younger version of yourself, offering advice on developing assertiveness. What lessons have you learned over the years?

8. Explore the role of assertiveness in setting and maintaining boundaries in relationships. How does assertive communication enhance mutual respect?

9. Imagine a world where everyone communicates assertively. How would this impact societal norms and interactions?

10. Write about a character who learns to assert themselves after years of passive behavior. What catalyzes this transformation, and what are the consequences?

11. Describe a conflict resolution scenario where assertiveness leads to a positive outcome for all parties involved.

12. Write a persuasive essay arguing the importance of teaching assertiveness skills in schools. How can assertiveness benefit students academically and socially?

13. Explore cultural differences in the expression of assertiveness. How does culture shape attitudes toward assertive behavior?

14. Write a short story where a character uses assertiveness to overcome a personal fear or obstacle. What lessons does the character learn about themselves?

15. Reflect on the role of self-esteem and assertiveness. How does healthy self-esteem contribute to assertive communication?

16. Describe a leadership situation where assertiveness was necessary to guide a team through a crisis or challenge.

17. Write a journal entry about a recent experience where you practiced assertiveness. What were the outcomes, and how did you feel afterward?

18. Explore the concept of assertive listening. How does actively listening to others' perspectives enhance assertive communication?

19. Write a dialogue between two friends discussing the importance of assertiveness in maintaining healthy friendships. How can assertiveness prevent misunderstandings and resentment?

20. Reflect on assertiveness as a lifelong skill. How can you continue to develop and refine your assertive communication skills in different areas of your life?

Practice Sheet for Assertiveness Techniques

All of the techniques we've learned don't mean very much if you don't use them in real life. Here, you'll find a log that you can use to document your successes and pain points when it comes to using your assertiveness with other people. Begin with basic assertion and practice it for a week or two before attempting other techniques. Focus on one technique at a time and use it whenever appropriate.

Keeping a small physical logbook or diary to record instances where you've employed these assertive techniques can be helpful, but you can also simply record memorable instances on your phone's notes app. This will allow you to track how frequently you are using assertiveness and identify which techniques are the most effective for you.

Here is a sample log sheet:

Date and Time	Technique Used	Situation and Details (How did you use the technique?)	Things to Remember for Next Time
Tuesday at 10 a.m.	"I" statement	When expressing myself to my boss, I used an "I" statement to communicate the additional materials I needed for my current project.	Next time, I'll try to make more direct eye contact.

Date and Time	Technique Used	Situation and Details (How did you use the technique?)	Things to Remember for Next Time

Positive Language Reframing Exercise

Positive communication styles and language greatly improve how couples perceive and interact with each other during conversations. Maintaining a positive tone is crucial, especially when discussing challenging topics, as it can have a significant impact on communication. The way something is communicated is often more important than the specific content, underscoring the importance of communication styles.

Conversely, negative language can lead to communication breakdowns, causing one partner to feel accused or attacked. Practicing positive language exercises involves consciously reframing statements to convey messages in a more supportive and affirming manner.

For instance, instead of saying, "Those pants don't look good on you," a more positive approach would be, "I loved those black pants you wore on our last date night." This simple adjustment not only avoids criticism but also reinforces appreciation and positivity within the relationship. By fostering positive communication habits, couples can strengthen their emotional connection and navigate difficulties with greater understanding and empathy.

To practice reframing, go through the following list of negatively framed statements and rewrite them positively. Remember to keep the core of the situation honest, and don't sidestep or make excuses.

Example:

"I don't like my job." versus "I'm exploring opportunities for a more fulfilling career."

1. "I'm always so forgetful."

2. "I can't handle stressful situations."

3. "I'll never get promoted."

4. "I'm not good at public speaking."

5. "I'm not as talented as my colleagues."

6. "I don't have enough time to relax."

7. "I hate Mondays."

8. "I never have enough money."

9. "I haven't been exercising enough lately."

10. "My spouse is being annoying right now."

Whenever you feel like something in your life isn't going your way, come back to this exercise. Write out the negative statements that frame the situation in a hopeless way, and then practice reframing the statements using positive language.

Simple Expression Exercise

Expressing emotions can sometimes feel challenging, especially if you're someone who struggles to open up or articulate your feelings fully. It's not uncommon for people to feel like they're shutting down and unable to find the right words to convey their emotions. Engaging in basic statement-making exercises can be instrumental in overcoming this communication barrier in the context of communication.

One effective technique involves identifying an emotion connected to a specific action or situation and then articulating it using structured statements. For instance, saying "I feel frustrated when you are late getting home" or "I feel disappointed when you cancel plans on me." This approach provides a framework for expressing emotions clearly and constructively, as well as giving you a baseline for putting words to your feelings. Through regular practice of identifying and vocalizing specific emotions, you can gradually enhance your ability to communicate your feelings more comfortably and authentically.

For this exercise, think about a current negative situation in your life. After considering it, write out 10 phrases using the template "I feel _ when _." Make sure to consider the full depth of how you felt as the situation progressed, and to reflect on all of the different aspects of the situation that might be triggering for you.

1. I feel _ when _.

2. I feel _ when _.

3. I feel _ when _.

4. I feel _ when _.

5. I feel _ when _.

6. I feel _ when _.

7. I feel _ when _.

8. I feel _ when _.

9. I feel _ when _.

10. I feel _ when _.

References

AbleGamers. (2024, May 7). *Role-Playing Games*. AbleGamers. https://ablegamers.org/role-playing-games/

Alpert, J. (2015, November 3). *7 Tips for Saying No Effectively*. Inc.com. https://www.inc.com/jonathan-alpert/7-ways-to-say-no-to-someone-and-not-feel-bad-about-it.html

American Psychiatric Association. (2020, March 5). *Psychiatry.org - Rumination: A Cycle of Negative Thinking*. Www.psychiatry.org. https://www.psychiatry.org/News-room/APA-Blogs/Rumination-A-Cycle-of-Negative-Thinking#:~:text=Rumination%20involves%20repetitive%20thinking%20or

Ames, D. (2009). Pushing up to a point: Assertiveness and effectiveness in leadership and interpersonal dynamics. *Research in Organizational Behavior*, *29*(2009), 111–133. https://doi.org/10.1016/j.riob.2009.06.010

Ames, D., Lee, A., & Wazlawek, A. (2017). Interpersonal assertiveness: inside the Balancing Act. *Social and Personality Psychology Compass*, *11*(6), e12317. https://doi.org/10.1111/spc3.12317

Anxiety and Depression Association of America. (2022, October 28). *Anxiety disorders - facts & statistics*. Anxiety and Depression Association of America; ADAA. https://adaa.org/understanding-anxiety/facts-statistics

Bacon, C. C., & Severson, M. L. (1986). Assertiveness, Responsiveness, and Versatility as Predictors of Leadership Emergence. *Communication Research Reports*, *3*(1), 53–59. https://doi.org/10.1080/17464099.1986.12289949

Baker, I. S., Turner, I. J., & Kotera, Y. (2022). Role-play Games (RPGs) for Mental Health (Why Not?): Roll for Initiative. *International Journal of Mental Health and Addiction*, *21*. https://doi.org/10.1007/s11469-022-00832-y

Bariso, J. (2016, February 11). *How Emotionally Intelligent People Handle Criticism: They Don't Do This*. Inc.com. https://www.inc.com/justin-bariso/how-emotionally-intelligent-people-handle-criticism-they-dont-do-this.html

Baumeister, R. F., Campbell, J. D., Krueger, J. I., & Vohs, K. D. (2003). Does High Self-Esteem Cause Better Performance, Interpersonal Success, Happiness, or Healthier Lifestyles? *Psychological Science in the Public Interest*, *4*(1), 1–44.

Better Health Channel. (2012). *Assertiveness*. Vic.gov.au. https://www.betterhealth.vic.gov.au/health/healthyliving/assertiveness

Billingham, A. (n.d.). *Talk yourself into being an assertive person - Skillset New Zealand*. Www.skillset.co.nz. Retrieved July 8, 2024, from https://www.skillset.co.nz/blog/alana-billingham-blog/28-people-skills/32-assertive-communication-skills

Blaschka, A. (2018). *Everything You've Ever Wanted Is Sitting On The Other Side Of Fear*. Forbes. https://www.forbes.com/sites/amyblaschka/2018/09/

04/everything-youve-ever-wanted-is-sitting-on-the-other-side-of-fear/

Boisvert, J.-M., Beaudry, M., & Bittar, J. (1985). Assertiveness training and human communication processes. *Journal of Contemporary Psychotherapy*, *15*(1), 58–73. https://doi.org/10.1007/bf00946127

Branson, R. (2020, January 15). *My Top tips for trying new things | Virgin*. Virgin.com. https://www.virgin.com/branson-family/richard-branson-blog/my-top-tips-trying-new-things

Broadwater, A. (2023, March 13). *Do You Text Your Grandkids? Read This Before Accidentally Making A Big Mistake*. HuffPost. https://www.huffpost.com/entry/texting-generational-differences_l_63f8db81e4b0cab1fa2eaa16

Caraniche At Work. (2017, November 21). *Assertiveness: a skill you might need to brush up on*. Caraniche. https://work.caraniche.com.au/assertiveness-a-skill-you-might-need-to-brush-up-on/#:~:text=Assertiveness%20is%20an%20interperso nal%20style

Center for Clinical Interventions. (2021). *Assertive communication*. Wa.gov.au. https://www.healthywa.wa.gov.au/Articles/A_E/Asse rtive-communication#:~:text=Assertiveness%20means%20e xpressing%20your%20point

Chaarani, B., Ortigara, J., Yuan, D., Loso, H., Potter, A., & Garavan, H. P. (2022). Association of Video Gaming With Cognitive Performance Among Children. *JAMA Network Open*, *5*(10), e2235721. https://doi.org/10.1001/jamanetworkopen.2022.35721

Chang, B. [Ben Chang]. (2018). For a lot of my life, I've been a very passive person, afraid to speak up when someone [Comment on the online forum post How can I stop being a passive person and become an assertive person]. Quora. https://www.quora.com/How-can-I-stop-being-a-passive-person-and-become-an-assertive-person

Chemaly, S. (2019, May 11). *How women and minorities are claiming their right to rage.* The Guardian. https://www.theguardian.com/lifeandstyle/2019/may/11/women-and-minorities-claiming-right-to-rage

Cherry, K. (2022a). *Locus of control and your life.* Verywell Mind. https://www.verywellmind.com/what-is-locus-of-control-2795434

Cherry, K. (2022b, May 13). *8 Signs You Might Be an Introvert.* Verywell Mind. https://www.verywellmind.com/signs-you-are-an-introvert-2795427#:~:text=While%20introverts%20make%20up%20an

Cherry, K. (2023, March 10). *Self-Awareness: How It Develops and Why It Matters.* Verywell Mind. https://www.verywellmind.com/what-is-self-awareness-2795023#:~:text=Self%2Dawareness%20is%20your%20ability

Clear, J. (2018). *Atomic Habits Archives.* James Clear. https://jamesclear.com/quote/atomic-habits

Cleveland Clinic. (2022, November 14). *Are Video Games Good for You?* Cleveland Clinic. https://health.clevelandclinic.org/are-video-games-good-for-you

Coburn, C. (2012). *Negotiation Conflict Styles.* https://hms.harvard.edu/sites/default/files/assets/Site s/Ombuds/files/NegotiationConflictStyles.pdf

Coursera Staff. (2023, January 17). *Assertive Communication: How to Do It (And Why It Matters).* Coursera. https://www.coursera.org/articles/assertive-communication

Coyne, S. M., Stockdale, L., & Summers, K. (2019). Problematic cell phone use, depression, anxiety, and self-regulation: Evidence from a three year longitudinal study from adolescence to emerging adulthood. *Computers in Human Behavior, 96,* 78–84. https://doi.org/10.1016/j.chb.2019.02.014

de Haan, R. (2019, February 21). *A habitually funny story.* Www.linkedin.com. https://www.linkedin.com/pulse/habitually-funny-story-robert-de-haan/

Desouky, D. E.-S., & Abu-Zaid, H. (2020). Mobile phone use pattern and addiction in relation to depression and anxiety. *Eastern Mediterranean Health Journal, 26*(6), 692–699. https://doi.org/10.26719/emhj.20.043

Eastern Washington University. (n.d.). *Self-Talk.* Inside.ewu.edu. https://inside.ewu.edu/calelearning/psychological-skills/self-talk/

Eatough, E. (2022, January 7). *How to say no to others (and why you shouldn't feel guilty).* BetterUp. https://www.betterup.com/blog/how-to-say-no

Eurich, T. (2018, January 4). *What self-awareness really is (and how to cultivate it).* Harvard Business Review; Harvard

Business Publishing. https://hbr.org/2018/01/what-self-awareness-really-is-and-how-to-cultivate-it

Eyal, N. (2023, January 4). *Labeling Yourself Is Keeping You Down, Do This Instead | Psychology Today*. Www.psychologytoday.com. https://www.psychologytoday.com/us/blog/automatic-you/202212/labeling-yourself-is-keeping-you-down-do-this-instead

Fields, R. D. (2019). The Roots of Human Aggression. *Scientific American*. https://doi.org/10.1038/scientificamerican0519-64

Garone, E. (2017, May 17). *Why we're different people at work and at home*. Www.bbc.com. https://www.bbc.com/worklife/article/20170518-why-were-different-people-at-work-and-at-home

Geisinger. (2017, November 28). *Why telling your teen to "calm down" is a bad idea*. Www.geisinger.org. https://www.geisinger.org/health-and-wellness/wellness-articles/2017/11/28/20/15/heres-why-telling-your-teen-to-calm-down-is-a-bad-idea

Glaab, S. (2022, April 11). *Council Post: How To Be More Assertive As A Leader*. Forbes. https://www.forbes.com/sites/forbescoachescouncil/2022/04/08/how-to-be-more-assertive-as-a-leader/

Godwin, J. (2020, September 20). *Let's Talk About… Assertiveness*. Let's Talk about Mental Health. https://letstalkaboutmentalhealth.com.au/2020/09/21/assertiveness/

Goman, C. K. (2016, March 31). Is Your Communication Style Dictated By Your Gender? *Forbes*. https://www.forbes.com/sites/carolkinseygoman/201

6/03/31/is-your-communication-style-dictated-by-your-gender/

Gu, H. J., Lee, O. S., & Hong, M. J. (2016). The Relationship between SNS addiction tendency, Self assertiveness, Interpersonal problems and in College students. *Journal of the Korea Academia-Industrial Cooperation Society*, *17*(4), 180–187. https://doi.org/10.5762/kais.2016.17.4.180

Hackman, R. (2016, July 12). *"It's like we're seen as animals": black men on their vulnerability and resilience*. The Guardian; The Guardian. https://www.theguardian.com/world/2016/jul/12/black-men-america-violence-vulnerable-detroit

Harris, J. (2018, October 10). *How to Handle Constructive Criticism in a Healthy Way*. Herzing University. https://www.herzing.edu/blog/how-handle-constructive-criticism-healthy-way

Harris, M. (2023, June 5). *The Pink Elephant Problem | Psychology Today*. Www.psychologytoday.com. https://www.psychologytoday.com/us/blog/letters-from-your-therapist/202303/the-pink-elephant-problem

Harrison, O. (2021, April 29). *I Thought I Knew My Boyfriend, Then I Met His Work Persona*. Www.refinery29.com. https://www.refinery29.com/en-us/2021/04/10450574/work-from-home-workplace-personas

Haupt, A. (2024, March 25). *Are Personality Tests Actually Useful?* TIME Magazine. https://time.com/6959682/are-personality-tests-useful/

Hewett, D., & Trinder, A. (2016). *Self-awareness, assertiveness & productive relationships.* https://www.ucl.ac.uk/~ucahdhe/F4.pdf

Hill, H. (2015, January 17). *Assertiveness - Improving your self-awareness.* Counselling in Your Community. https://inyourcommunity.org.uk/2015/01/17/assertiv eness-improving-self-awareness/

Hughs, T. (2015, January 22). *Lost In Translation. Funny True Miscommunication.* Www.linkedin.com. https://www.linkedin.com/pulse/lost-translation-funny-true-miscommunication-tony-j-hughes/

Kaur, G. K., & S.K., M. (2015). Correlation of Assertive Behavior with Communication Satisfaction among Nurses. *Journal of Health, Medicine and Nursing, 14.* ResearchGate.net. https://www.researchgate.net/profile/Dr-S-K-Maheshwari/publication/309242133_Correlation_of_A ssertive_Behavior_with_Communication_Satisfaction_a mong_Nurses/links/580709ac08ae03256b770037/Corr elation-of-Assertive-Behavior-with-Communication-Satisfaction-among-Nurses.pdf

Keates, C. (2022). Students' experience of the challenges of using assertive communication. *British Journal of Nursing, 31*(15), 790–798. https://doi.org/10.12968/bjon.2022.31.15.790

Keohan, E. (2021, November 24). *17 Communicaton Exercises for Couples Therapy.* Talkspace. https://www.talkspace.com/blog/communication-exercises-for-couples-therapy/#:~:text=An%20easy%20way%20to%20practi ce

Keturka, J., & Laurinavicius, R. (2020, September 3). *30 Times People Misunderstood Each Other And Hilarity Ensued.* Bored Panda. https://www.boredpanda.com/funny-misunderstanding-tweets/

Killion, R. (2017, July 31). *Imaginary Conversations.* Lifevise. https://lifevise.com/imaginary-conversations/

Kluger, J. (2017). 7 Signs You're Dealing With a Passive-Aggressive Person. In *Time.* https://time.com/4916056/passive-aggressive-definition-meaning/

Kozak, A. (2014, April 3). *There Is No Such Thing as an Introvert or Extrovert | Psychology Today.* Www.psychologytoday.com. https://www.psychologytoday.com/us/blog/the-buddha-was-introvert/201404/there-is-no-such-thing-introvert-or-extrovert

Lane, C. (2009). The Surprising History of Passive-Aggressive Personality Disorder. *Theory & Psychology, 19*(1), 55–70. https://doi.org/10.1177/0959354308101419

Lapakko, D. (2007). Communication Is 93% Nonverbal: an Urban Legend Proliferates. *Communication and Theater Association of Minnesota Journal, 34*(2), 7–19. https://cornerstone.lib.mnsu.edu/cgi/viewcontent.cgi?article=1000&context=ctamj

Laud, R. L., & Johnson, M. (2012). Upward mobility. *Career Development International, 17*(3), 231–254. https://doi.org/10.1108/13620431211241072

Lazenby, C.-L. (2015). *Assertiveness and leadership perceptions: The role of gender and Leader-Member Exchange.* https://www.proquest.com/openview/bf9432cb73f7b7cf974e3271bf6a7b0b/1?pq-origsite=gscholar&cbl=18750

Lilienfeld, S. O., Sauvigné, K. C., Lynn, S. J., Cautin, R. L., Latzman, R. D., & Waldman, I. D. (2015). Fifty psychological and psychiatric terms to avoid: a list of inaccurate, misleading, misused, ambiguous, and logically confused words and phrases. *Frontiers in Psychology*, *6*(2015). https://doi.org/10.3389/fpsyg.2015.01100

Lindsay, N. (2017, September 29). *Taking Constructive Criticism Like a Champ*. Themuse.com; The Muse. https://www.themuse.com/advice/taking-constructive-criticism-like-a-champ

Lonczak, H. S. (2020, September 3). *What is Assertive Communication? 10 Real-Life Examples*. PositivePsychology.com. https://positivepsychology.com/assertive-communication/#characteristics

Long, J. (2019, July 1). *Avoidance: The Band-Aid Solution to Long-Term Problems*. The Psychology Group Fort Lauderdale. https://thepsychologygroup.com/avoidance/#:~:text=Avoidance%20is%20a%20maladaptive%20coping

Makin, S. (2024, July 5). *Not Everyone Has an Inner Voice Streaming Through Their Head*. Scientific American. https://www.scientificamerican.com/article/not-everyone-has-an-inner-voice-streaming-through-their-head/

Markid, M., Khorami Markani, A., Radfar, M., & Khalkhali, H. (2019). *The effect of assertiveness-based intervention program on self- esteem and interpersonal communication skills in nursing students.* https://japer.in/storage/models/article/I95LBcTSarsnrT7wGt3QM7680mKo85hlWfRJWpRpr93tbRFmlI0jt1v9BQ1C/the-effect-of-assertiveness-based-intervention-program-on-self-esteem-and-interpersonal-communicat.pdf

Martins, J. (2022, July 18). *How to Give and Take Constructive Criticism • Asana.* Asana. https://asana.com/resources/constructive-criticism

Masters, H. (2023, January 18). *Aggressive and assertiveness: the fine line for women in leadership.* DiversityQ. https://diversityq.com/women-in-leadership-the-fine-line-between-aggressive-and-assertive/

Maurer, R. (2021, July 5). *Resistance to Change | Why it Matters and What to Do About It?* Rick Maurer. https://rickmaurer.com/articles/resistance-to-change-why-it-matters/

Mayo Clinic Staff. (2020, May 29). *Being assertive: Reduce stress, communicate better.* Mayo Clinic. https://www.mayoclinic.org/healthy-lifestyle/stress-management/in-depth/assertive/art-20044644

McCormick-Huhn, K., & Shields, S. (2021). Favorable Evaluations of Black and White Women's Workplace Anger During the Era of #MeToo. *Frontiers, 12*(2021). https://doi.org/10.3389/fpsyg.2021.594260

McHugh, C. (2013). The art of being yourself | Caroline McHugh | TEDxMiltonKeynesWomen [YouTube Video]. In *YouTube.* https://www.youtube.com/watch?v=veEQQ-N9xWU

McLeod, L. E. (2012, February 21). *Are You Aggressive or Assertive? Frantic or Focused?* HuffPost. https://www.huffpost.com/entry/aggressive-assertive_b_1289183

Merriam-Webster. (n.d.-a). Assertive. In *Merriam-Webster.com dictionary*. Retrieved July 11, 2024, 2020, from https://www.merriam-webster.com/dictionary/semantics

Merriam-Webster. (n.d.-b). Passive. In *Merriam-Webster.com dictionary*. Retrieved July 11, 2024,, from https://www.merriam-webster.com/dictionary/semantics

Merriam-Webster. (n.d.-c). Aggressive. In *Merriam-Webster.com dictionary*. Retrieved July 11, 2024,, 2020, from https://www.merriam-webster.com/dictionary/semantics

Meyer, M. (n.d.). *The Why Behind Procrastination | NTC Student Success*. Success.tulane.edu. https://success.tulane.edu/why-behind-procrastination#:~:text=According%20to%20research%20from%20the

Michail, J. (2020, August 24). *Council Post: Strong Nonverbal Skills Matter Now More Than Ever In This "New Normal."* Forbes. https://www.forbes.com/sites/forbescoachescouncil/2020/08/24/strong-nonverbal-skills-matter-now-more-than-ever-in-this-new-normal/

Mind. (2022, August). *About self-esteem*. Www.mind.org.uk. https://www.mind.org.uk/information-support/types-of-mental-health-problems/self-esteem/about-self-esteem/#:~:text=Self%2Desteem%20is%20how%20we

Motro, D., Evans, J. B., Ellis, A. P. J., & Benson III, L. (2022, January 31). *The "Angry Black Woman" Stereotype at Work*. Harvard Business Review.

https://hbr.org/2022/01/the-angry-black-woman-stereotype-at-work

National Institute of Mental Health. (2017). *NIMH: Social Anxiety Disorder*. Www.nimh.nih.gov. https://www.nimh.nih.gov/health/statistics/social-anxiety-disorder

newroads. (2022, August 8). *The Importance of Being Self Aware -*. New Roads Behavioral Health. https://newroadstreatment.org/the-importance-of-being-self-awareness/

Orth, U., & Robins, R. W. (2021, July 28). *APA PsycNet*. Psycnet.apa.org. https://psycnet.apa.org/fulltext/2022-48842-002.html

Oxford English Dictionary. (2023). Assertiveness. In *Oxford English Dictionary*. https://www.oed.com/dictionary/assertiveness_n?tl=true

Paulise, L. (2023, November 7). *Why You Need To Speak Up: 3 Ways To Master Assertiveness At Work*. Forbes. https://www.forbes.com/sites/lucianapaulise/2023/11/07/why-you-need-to-speak-up-3-ways-to-master-assertiveness-at-work/

Psychology Today Staff. (2019). *Assertiveness | Psychology Today*. Psychology Today. https://www.psychologytoday.com/us/basics/assertiveness

Rogers, C., & Schainker, L. (n.d.). *Using Active Listening to Enhance Your Relationships*. Extension.usu.edu. https://extension.usu.edu/relationships/faq/using-active-listening-to-enhance-your-relationships#:~:text=Typically%2C%20when%20we%20actively%20listen

Rosenthal, R., & Jacobson, L. (1968). *Pygmalion in the Classroom : Teacher Expectation and pupils' Intellectual Development.* Holt, Rinehart and Winston.

Schaffner, A. K. (2021, July 7). *Define or Be Defined: On Self-Labelling | Psychology Today.* Www.psychologytoday.com. https://www.psychologytoday.com/us/blog/the-art-of-self-improvement/202107/define-or-be-defined-on-self-labelling

Schenker, M. (2022, April 30). *How to Use Cialdini's 6 Principles of Persuasion to Boost Conversions.* CXL. https://cxl.com/blog/cialdinis-principles-persuasion/#h-2-commitment-people-want-their-beliefs-to-be-consistent-with-their-values

Scott, E. (2023, December 6). *How to Say No to People in 3 Simple Steps.* Verywell Mind. https://www.verywellmind.com/say-no-to-people-making-demands-on-your-time-3145025

Selby, J. (2021, July 7). *Aggressive Or Assertive? What To Do If You're Labe... | Edit.* AllBright. https://www.allbrightcollective.com/edit/articles/aggressive-or-assertive-what-to-do-if-youre-labelled-at-work

Sells, N. (2021, January 26). *Reasons to See a Therapist.* Davis Behavioral Health. https://www.dbhutah.org/reasons-to-see-a-therapist/

Smith, E. E. (2015, April 23). *Mixed Signals: Why People Misunderstand Each Other.* The Atlantic. https://www.theatlantic.com/health/archive/2015/04/mixed-signals-why-people-misunderstand-each-other/391053/

Spector, N. (2019, November 6). *What is self-awareness? And how can you cultivate it?* NBC News. https://www.nbcnews.com/better/lifestyle/what-self-awareness-how-can-you-cultivate-it-ncna1067721

StopItNow.org. (n.d.). *Self esteem and assertiveness.* Stop It Now. https://www.stopitnow.org.uk/concerned-about-your-own-thoughts-or-behavior/help-with-inappropriate-thoughts-or-behavior/self-help/your-well-being-and-self-care/self-esteem-and-assertiveness/#:~:text=People%20with%20low%20self%2Desteem

trainmax. [trainmax]. (2023). Work in IT. Been the free IT-Guy to fix or setup Phones, Computers, Websites or even TVs, first for my family... Then for my friends... Then for their friends. For Years. Couldn't say no. [Comment on the online forum post How to say "no" to people?]. Reddit. https://www.reddit.com/r/ask/comments/16arg42/how_to_say_no_to_people/

Travers, M. (2023, March 28). *A Psychologist Teaches You How To Be More Assertive In Your Relationship.* Forbes. https://www.forbes.com/sites/traversmark/2023/03/28/a-psychologist-teaches-you-how-to-be-more-assertive-in-your-relationship/

Trepany, C. (2024, June 27). *TikTok is shocked at these hilarious, unhinged text messages from boomer parents.* USA TODAY. https://www.usatoday.com/story/life/health-wellness/2024/06/27/tiktok-of-ominous-text-messages-from-parents-goes-viral-watch/74228679007/

Tulgan, B. (2020, September 1). *Learn When to Say No.* Harvard Business Review. https://hbr.org/2020/09/learn-when-to-say-no

Uthaman, T. (2024, April 28). The Art of Saying "No" and Other Stories. *ThendralUthaman.com.* https://www.thendraluthaman.com/blog/the-art-of-saying-no-and-other-stories

van Doren, C. (2023, March 23). *Dungeons & downtime: how tabletop roleplaying games benefit college students - The Arizona State Press.* Www.statepress.com. https://www.statepress.com/article/2023/03/rpg-escapism-appeal#

Vankar, P. (2024, March 22). *Mental health treatment or therapy among U.S. adults 2022.* Statista. https://www.statista.com/statistics/794027/mental-health-treatment-counseling-past-year-us-adults/#:~:text=2002%2D2022&text=In%202022%2C%20around%2055.8%20million

Vedantam, S. (2017, December 11). *How Labels Can Affect People's Personalities And Potential.* NPR.org. https://www.npr.org/2017/12/11/569983801/how-labels-can-affect-peoples-personalities-and-potential

Višnjić, A., Veličković, V., Sokolović, D., Stanković, M., Mijatović, K., Stojanović, M., Milošević, Z., & Radulović, O. (2018). Relationship between the Manner of Mobile Phone Use and Depression, Anxiety, and Stress in University Students. *International Journal of Environmental Research and Public Health, 15*(4), 697. https://doi.org/10.3390/ijerph15040697

Weill, A. [Andrew Weill]. (2023). My wife could have written this question, about 29 years ago. At that time, I was hugely defensive if criticized [Comment on the online forum post I have a problem with my relationship. I can't say anything critical (constructive criticism), I can't even speak out when my partner does something wrong that hurt my feelings, without him getting mad. What can I do about this situation?] Quora. https://www.quora.com/I-have-a-problem-with-my-relationship-I-can-t-say-anything-critical-constructive-criticism-I-can-t-even-speak-out-when-my-partner-does-something-wrong-that-hurt-my-feelings-without-him-getting-mad-What-can-I-do

Wright, C. N., & Roloff, M. E. (2015). You Should Just Know Why I'm Upset: Expectancy Violation Theory and the Influence of Mind Reading Expectations (MRE) on Responses to Relational Problems. *Communication Research Reports, 32*(1), 10–19. https://doi.org/10.1080/08824096.2014.989969

Image References

Adriane, M. (2017). good vibes only text. In *Unsplash*. https://unsplash.com/photos/good-vibes-only-text-muS2RraYRuQ

Ahmed, E. (2017). close-up photography of brown wooden card catalog. In *Unsplash*. https://unsplash.com/photos/close-up-photography-of-brown-wooden-card-catalog-Y3KEBQlB1Zk

Brandsma, S. (2020). Brown wooden blocks with numbers. In *Unsplash*. https://unsplash.com/photos/brown-wooden-blocks-with-numbers-C5SUkYZT7nU

Child, B. (2015). Oval brown wooden conference table and chairs inside conference room. In *Unsplash*. https://unsplash.com/photos/oval-brown-wooden-conference-table-and-chairs-inside-conference-room-GWe0dlVD9e0

Czerwinski, P. (2021). White and black number print on blue textile. In *Unsplash*. https://unsplash.com/photos/white-and-black-number-print-on-blue-textile-7dVBX9ecSzQ

Gerry, C. (2023). A display in a mall filled with lots of signs. In *Unsplash*. https://unsplash.com/photos/a-display-in-a-mall-filled-with-lots-of-signs-QSyl2KVys0s

Hoehne, J. (2021). text. In *Unsplash*. https://unsplash.com/photos/text-YPgTovTiUv4

Hou, D. (2020). Red and white no smoking sign. In *Unsplash*. https://unsplash.com/photos/red-and-white-no-smoking-sign-BjD3KhnTIkg

Hudson, D. (2020). brown wicker basket on white table. In *Unsplash*. https://unsplash.com/photos/brown-wicker-basket-on-white-table-TqKFiMR9O6s

Koycheva, E. (2018). fortune cookie. In *Unsplash*. https://unsplash.com/photos/fortune-cookie-GUYCM0jhuSA

Mossholder, T. (2021). A wooden floor with a yellow sign with a picture of a pair of feet., In *Unsplash*. https://unsplash.com/photos/a-wooden-floor-with-a-yellow-sign-with-a-picture-of-a-pair-of-feet-fxB2UAO0dcY

Muhammad, E. (2023). A computer keyboard on an orange background. In *Unsplash*.

https://unsplash.com/photos/a-computer-keyboard-on-an-orange-background-9oPvRKuiO5Q

Nik. (2021). yellow and white round plastic toy. In *Unsplash*. https://unsplash.com/photos/yellow-and-white-round-plastic-toy-zYdYz7JlevE

Sharma, R. (2020). Black ipad on brown wooden table. In *Unsplash*. https://unsplash.com/photos/black-ipad-on-brown-wooden-table-RnW1taVZqm8

Spiske, M. (2018). brown game pieces on white surface. In *Unsplash*. https://unsplash.com/photos/brown-game-pieces-on-white-surface-QozzJpFZ2lg

Tabitha. (2021). Photo of White Daisy Flowers in Front of a Mirror. In *Pexels*. https://www.pexels.com/photo/photo-of-white-daisy-flowers-in-front-of-a-mirror-8660680/

Tyson, J. (2019). No sign photo. In *Unsplash*. https://unsplash.com/photos/no-sign-2TzSuQZOHe4

Vignes, R. (2015). focus dictionary index page. In *Unsplash*. https://unsplash.com/photos/focus-dictionary-index-page-ywqa9IZB-dU

wuz. (2018). Selective Focus Photography of Dynamic Microphone. In *Unsplash*. https://unsplash.com/photos/selective-focus-photography-of-dynamic-microphone-1G6CHyxIxMI

Hey, You! Yes, You!

You made it to the end – high five!

If this book gave you an "aha!" moment or even a chuckle, I've got a tiny favor to ask: could you *pretty please* leave a review on Amazon? It's like giving the book a virtual hug, and it helps others find it too!

And hey, if you think someone else could use a boost, share this book with them. You'll be their hero (and mine too)!

Thanks a bunch,

Linton J. Khor

P.S. The review doesn't have to be a masterpiece—just a few kind words will do!

If you want to follow this work, see more about me and other projects drop by at:

nwnlab.co

Made in the USA
Las Vegas, NV
02 December 2024